RAND McNALLY
ILLUSTRATED ATLAS OF TODAY'S WORLD

VOLUME 1

UNITED STATES I *Alabama–Michigan*

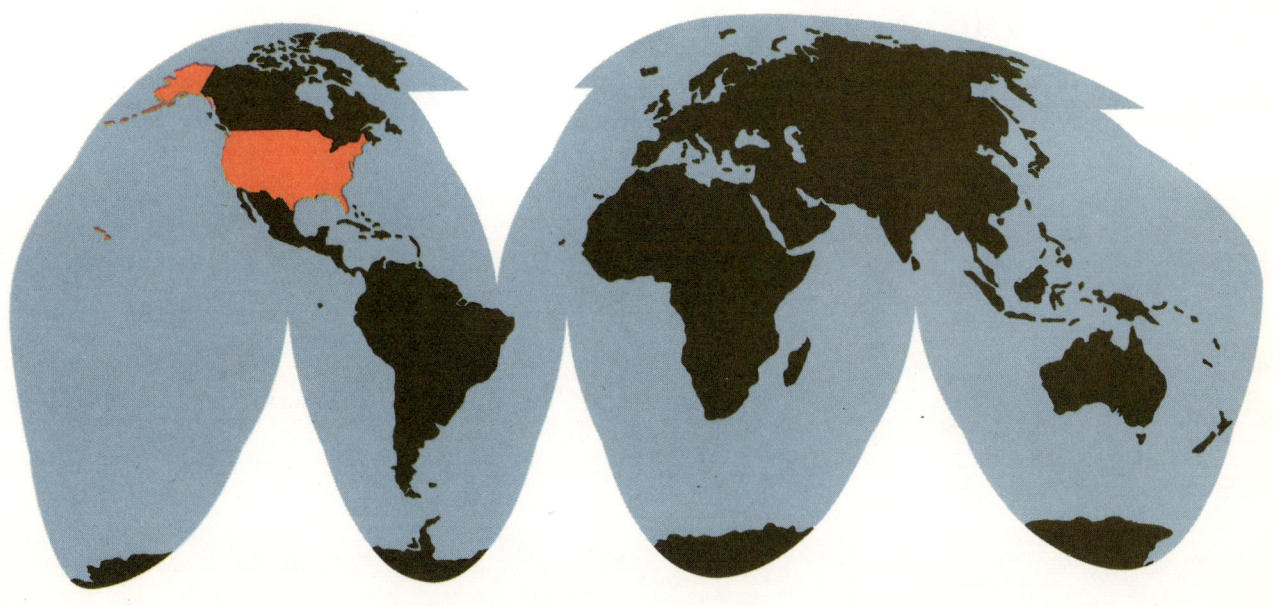

RAND McNALLY & COMPANY   NEW YORK / CHICAGO / SAN FRANCISCO

ADVISORY BOARD

Fred W. Foster, Ph. D.
Professor of Geography
University of Illinois

Hans Morgenthau, Ph. D.
Professor of Political Science
and History
University of Chicago

J. Lewis Robinson, Ph. D.
Professor of Geography and
Chairman of the Department
University of British Columbia

STAFF

Editor-Text
Lewis W. Gillenson

Writers
Donald Allen
Stanley H. Brown
Caroline Byass
Eugene Dunlop
Darlene Geis
Peggy Lampl
David Landman
Frank Latham
Leonard Louis Levinson
Alan Littell
Hubert Pryor

Managing Editor
Dolores Field

Associate Editor
Helen Harter

Copy Editor
Ann Bishop

Cartography
The Cartographic
Staff of
Rand McNally
& Company

Art Director
Chris J. Arvetis

Designer
Gordon Hartshorne

Layout
Mario Pagliai
Terry Rose

Picture Editor
Alice P. Galway

Illustrations
Charles Moser

1971 Edition
Copyright © MCMLXII by Rand McNally & Company
All Rights Reserved   Printed in U.S.A.

CONTENTS

A Note to Our Readers 8

1 THE UNITED STATES: PART I . . . 11

Alabama	24	Delaware	48	Kansas	74
Alaska	27	Florida	50	Kentucky	78
Arizona	30	Georgia	54	Louisiana	82
Arkansas	33	Hawaii	57	Maine	85
California	36	Idaho	60	Maryland	88
Colorado	40	Illinois	64	Massachusetts	91
Connecticut	44	Indiana	68	Michigan	94
		Iowa	71		

2 THE UNITED STATES: PART II . . . 97

Minnesota	100	New York	130	Tennessee	162
Mississippi	104	North Carolina	134	Texas	166
Missouri	107	North Dakota	137	Utah	170
Montana	110	Ohio	140	Vermont	173
Nebraska	113	Oklahoma	144	Virginia	176
Nevada	116	Oregon	148	Washington	180
New Hampshire . . .	119	Pennsylvania	151	West Virginia	184
New Jersey	122	Rhode Island	154	Wisconsin	187
New Mexico	126	South Carolina	156	Wyoming	190
		South Dakota	159		

3 NORTHERN AND WESTERN EUROPE: . . . 193

British Isles	209	Denmark	239	Belgium	262
United Kingdom . . .	212	Finland	241	Netherlands	267
Ireland	224	Iceland	244	Germany	269
Northern Europe . . .	229	**Western Europe** . . .	247	Austria	280
Norway	232	France	250	Liechtenstein	282
Sweden	235	Monaco	260	Switzerland	283
		Luxembourg	261		

4 SOUTHERN AND EASTERN EUROPE AND THE SOVIET UNION: . . . 289

Southern Europe . . .	293	Vatican City	322	Yugoslavia	340
Portugal	302	San Marino	323	Romania	344
Spain	308	Malta	323	Hungary	347
Andorra	313	Greece	325	Czechoslovakia . . .	350
Gibraltar	313	Albania	331	Poland	357
Italy	314	**Eastern Europe** . . .	333	**The Soviet Union** . . .	363
		Bulgaria	336		

5 THE MIDDLE EAST AND NORTH AFRICA: 385

Arabian Peninsula . . . 397	**Iran and Afghanistan** . . . 417	United Arab Republic
Saudi Arabia 398	Iran 420	(Egypt) 454
Yemen 402	Afghanistan 424	Libya 460
Southern Yemen . . . 404	**Eastern Mediterranean** . . . 429	Tunisia 463
Muscat and Oman . . . 405	Turkey 432	**Northwest Africa** 467
Trucial States 405	Cyprus 437	Algeria 470
Qatar 406	Syria 438	Morocco 474
Bahrain 408	Lebanon 441	Canary Islands 478
Kuwait 409	Israel 443	Madeira Islands 480
Iraq 411	Jordan 448	Azores 480
	Northeast Africa 451	

6 AFRICA SOUTH OF THE SAHARA: 481

Southern Africa 491	Republic of the Congo	Togo 550
Republic of South Africa . . 494	(Kinshasa) 524	Ghana 551
South West Africa . . . 499	**Equatorial Africa** 529	Liberia 554
Lesotho 499	Republic of the Congo	Sierra Leone 556
Swaziland 501	(Brazzaville) 532	Guinea 557
Botswana 501	Equatorial Guinea . . . 533	Portuguese Guinea . . . 558
Malagasy Republic . . . 502	Gabon 534	Mali 558
Central Africa 505	Central African Republic . 535	Gambia 560
Mozambique 508	Chad 536	Senegal 561
Rhodesia 509	Cameroon 536	Mauritania 562
Zambia 512	**West Africa** 539	Spanish Sahara 563
Malawi 513	Nigeria 542	Cape Verde Islands . . . 563
Angola 514	Niger 546	**East Africa** 565
Tanzania 515	Dahomey 548	Somali Republic 568
Kenya 519	Upper Volta 549	Afars and Issas . . . 569
Uganda 523	Ivory Coast 549	Ethiopia 570
Rwanda and Burundi . . 523		Sudan 573

7 EASTERN AND SOUTHERN ASIA: 577

Eastern Asia 587	Philippines 620	Vietnam 642
Japan 590	Indonesia 626	**South Central Asia** . . . 647
Korea 599	Portuguese Timor . . . 630	Burma 650
Mongolia 602	Brunei 631	Bhutan 653
China 603	Singapore 631	Sikkim 653
Taiwan (Formosa) . . . 612	Malaysia 634	Nepal 655
Hong Kong 614	Thailand 636	Pakistan 656
Macao 614	Cambodia 640	India 662
Southeastern Asia 617	Laos 641	Ceylon 670

8 CANADA: 673

Atlantic Provinces . . . 687
   Nova Scotia 690
   New Brunswick 695
   Prince Edward Island . . . 698
   Newfoundland 701
Middle Provinces 707

Quebec 710
Ontario 720
Western Provinces 731
   Manitoba 734
   Saskatchewan 740

Alberta 747
British Columbia 752
Northern Canada 761
   Yukon 762
   Northwest Territories . . . 765

9 LATIN AMERICA: 769

Middle America 779
   Mexico 782
   Guatemala 792
   Honduras 793
   British Honduras 793
   El Salvador 794
   Nicaragua 794
   Costa Rica 795
   Panama 796
   Cuba 800

Bahamas 802
Haiti 803
Dominican Republic . . . 804
Jamaica 805
Caribbean Islands . . . 806
Puerto Rico 810
Virgin Islands 813
Northern South America . 815
Brazil 818
Guianas 826

Venezuela 830
Colombia 835
Ecuador 840
Peru 842
Bolivia 845
Southern South America . 847
Chile 850
Paraguay 853
Uruguay 856
Argentina 858

10 AUSTRALIA, OCEANIA, AND POLAR REGIONS: 865

Australia and New Zealand . 869
   Australia 874
   New Zealand 884
The Oceans 895

Atlantic Ocean 903
Indian Ocean 911
Monsoon Winds 914
Pacific Ocean 917

Pacific Islands 927
Polar Regions 939
Arctic Ocean 943
Antarctic 950

11 OUR WORLD: 961

World Population 965
World Transportation . . . 977
Languages of the World . . 993
Races of the World . . . 999

Religions of the World . . 1007
Natural Vegetation . . . 1015
Climates of the World . . 1023

Landforms 1029
Reference Tables 1050
Glossary 1055

12 GUIDE TO TODAY'S WORLD: 1057

Map Symbols

POLITICAL BOUNDARIES

International
State and Provincial
County

CITIES, TOWNS AND VILLAGES

Size of symbol indicates the population of the place.

Size of type indicates the relative importance of the place

Corporate areas of large U.S. and Canadian cities and urban areas of other foreign cities.

Major Urban Areas (Area of continuous commercial, industrial and residential development in and around a major city)

Capital Cities

County Seats are indicated by dot-centered symbol.

Community within a city

Scientific station

Military installation

MISCELLANEOUS

National Parks, Monuments, and Indian Reservations.

Railroads
Ruins
Dikes
Bridges
Dams
Canals

PHYSICAL FEATURES

Ranges
Peaks
Passes — SOUTH PASS
Point of Elevation above sea level (in feet) — 7,268 FT.
Escarpments, Bluffs Cliffs and Plateaus — PLATEAU
Glaciers
Volcanoes
Lava Flows
Sand Dunes
Deserts
Swamps and Marshes

Explanation of the Index Reference System, page 9.

RAND McNALLY ILLUSTRATED ATLAS OF TODAY'S WORLD

Moscow

Grand Canyon, Arizona

Tokyo

Latin America

A Note to Our Readers

Do you sometimes wish that you could discuss world events more knowledgeably?

Would your son or daughter appreciate a study aid that would give him invaluable help with his social studies, geography, history, or current events assignment at school?

The Rand McNally ILLUSTRATED ATLAS OF TODAY'S WORLD has been designed by the world's leading mapmaker to help you and your family learn more about the world of the 1970's.

While it is called an atlas, it is much more than that. It includes not only the finest quality Rand McNally maps, but also many carefully selected photographs and easy-to-read articles.

You'll find the ILLUSTRATED ATLAS a convenient way to keep up-to-date on the many new nations of Africa and Asia, on changing forms of government, and on the geographical, historical, and economic background of each nation.

For your convenience, the ILLUSTRATED ATLAS is divided into separate volumes as follows:

1. The United States: Part I.
2. The United States: Part II.
3. Northern and Western Europe.
4. Southern and Eastern Europe and the Soviet Union.
5. The Middle East and North Africa.
6. Africa South of the Sahara.
7. Eastern and Southern Asia.
8. Canada.
9. Latin America.
10. Australia, Oceania, and the Polar Regions.
11. Our World, a discussion of the world's peoples, their races, languages, and religions, and the natural setting in which they live.
12. Guide to Today's World, listing the nations and leading cities of the world, with page references to indexed maps of the nations in the ILLUSTRATED ATLAS. Also included are numerous city maps and photographs of leading cities of the world.

At the introduction to each volume, you'll find a handy alphabetical list of the nations in that volume, plus an index to that volume's maps. The marginal indexing system used with the maps is described on the opposite page.

Accompanying the maps of each nation is an updated discussion of its geography, history, and economics. In addition, there is a fact block giving an up-to-date population estimate, the nation's area, language, religion, and other facts. Each nation's flag is reproduced in color.

A realization of the need for every citizen to know and understand the world in which he lives has been our challenge in creating this set of books.

You'll find the ILLUSTRATED ATLAS OF TODAY'S WORLD a unique educational aid for all members of the family. Its up-to-the-minute, detailed maps are equal or superior to those in much more expensive works; mass distribution makes its modest cost possible.

1 United States I

2 United States II

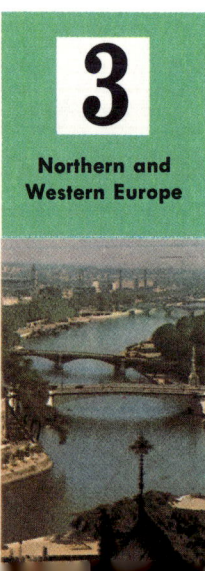
3 Northern and Western Europe

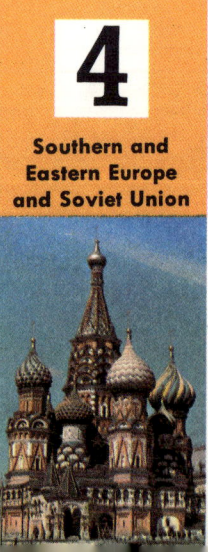
4 Southern and Eastern Europe and Soviet Union

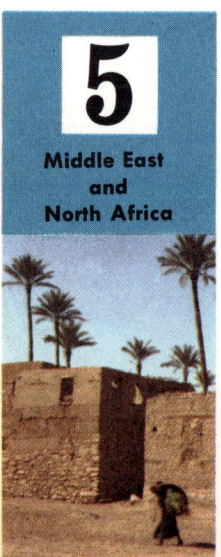
5 Middle East and North Africa

6 Africa South of the Sahara

Introduction / 9

EXPLANATION OF THE INDEX REFERENCE SYSTEM

The sample map and index below show how to use the index to find cities and towns on the maps in these pages. In most sections physical features are indexed on the continent maps. The cities and towns for each political unit are listed in alphabetical order. Following the name of the city is a CAPITAL letter and a number. In the sample index below, the name "Helsinki" is followed by "C12." The CAPITAL letters in the index refer to letters that appear on the left and right margins of most of the maps. These letters are placed *between* numbered blue lines that go from east to west and indicate degrees of latitude. The numbers in the index refer to numbers that appear on the upper and lower margins of most of the maps *between* numbered blue lines that go from north to south and indicate degrees of longitude. The two sets of blue lines cross on the map and divide it into "boxes." Note that on some maps the boxes are NOT squares, because the horizontal lines may curve and the vertical lines may be closer together north or south than they are near the equator. To locate Helsinki on the sample map, find the box formed by the blue lines above and below the letter C in the left and right margins, and the blue lines to the left and right of the figure 12 in the top and bottom margins. The symbol for Helsinki is somewhere within this box.

Some maps have small insets showing cities or areas in greater detail, or showing islands or other features. Locations on these insets are indicated in the index by a small letter and a number (e14).

On the map, the names of cities with large populations are printed in larger type than the names of cities with small populations. Names of physical features, such as rivers, lakes, and mountains, are printed in *italic* type, and political divisions are in large CAPITAL letters.

⊛ **Capitals**

Helsinki, Fin	C12
Moscow, Sov. Un	D15
Oslo, Nor	D10
Stockholm, Swe	D11

Physical Features

Ahvenanmaa, is	C11
Beloye, lake	C15
Bothnia, gulf	C12
Dvinskaya, bay	B15
Finland, gulf	C13
Inari, lake	B13
Indalsälven, riv	C11
Kandalakshskaya, bay	B14
Kanin, cape	B16
Kemijoki, riv	B13
Kola, pen	B15
Ladoga, lake	C14
Lofoten, is	B10
Lovat, riv	D14
Mälaren, lake	D11
Mezen, riv	C17
Mezenskaya, bay	B16
Msta, riv	D14
Muonio, riv	B12
North, cape	A13
Northern Dvina, riv	C16
Onega, lake	C15
Onega, riv	C15
Peipus, lake	D13
Pskov, lake	D13
Riga, gulf	D12
Rybinsk, res	D15
Siljan, lake	C10
Storavan, lake	B11
Sukhona, riv	D16
Tanaelv, riv	A13
Torneträsk, lake	B12
Tuloma, riv	B14
Umeälven, riv	C11
Vänern, lake	D10
Vättern, lake	D10
Vesterålen, is	B10
Vestfjorden, fjord	B10
White, sea	B15

7 Eastern and Southern Asia

8 Canada

9 Latin America

10 Australia, Oceania, and Polar Regions

11 Our World

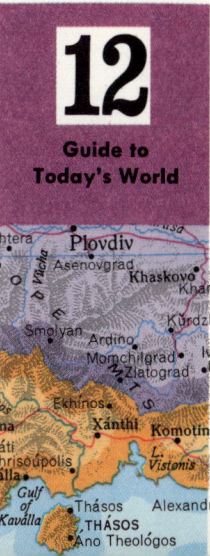

12 Guide to Today's World

A Titan rocket with manned Gemini space capsule leaves launching pad at Cape Kennedy.

The Enchanted Castle in Disneyland, Anaheim, California.

RAND McNALLY
ILLUSTRATED ATLAS
OF TODAY'S WORLD

THE UNITED STATES
Part I

Mount Rushmore, South Dakota

Introduction to
UNITED STATES
PART I

United States I

There are many ways of learning to know the United States. The pioneers who traveled across it on foot or in ox-drawn wagons learned about its size, its weather, its rivers, plains, and mountains almost inch by inch. Today it is possible to cross the country, from the shores of one great ocean to the other, driving over mountains on four-lane highways, and speeding over the wide plains in days, not months. The truck drivers, tourists, salesmen—all the travelers who cross the land by automobile—learn to know the country mile by mile rather than inch by inch, and much of it is quite different from what the pioneers saw, for the land has been changed.

There was a time, while America was wild and natural, that an Indian, so it is said, could have walked halfway across the continent, had he chosen to, without ever leaving the shelter of a tree. Most of that great woodland is gone. The trees have been cut and the land cleared; cities, towns, and roads have been built, and crops have been planted. The early explorers of the West crossed a sea of grass. The grass is gone now, and so are the great herds of buffalo, and the Indians that hunted them. In the spring the prairies are no longer one vast garden of wild flowers, and there are few places left where, in the fall, the numberless flights of migrating birds really darken the sky. The grass has given way to wheat, corn, cotton, and hay; herds of steers and sheep graze the range lands; cities now rise where once the swamplands fed and sheltered the wild birds. The changes in the land have made the United States a great and powerful nation, capable of feeding, clothing, and housing a tremendous population, of providing them with machines, and weapons, and toys, and education. None of this would be possible if it were not for the mines, the wheat fields, the dams that hold the rivers back, but still, not all the changes are good. Every resource, no matter how endless it seems, can be depleted, and nothing in nature that is greatly changed can ever be restored to its original state.

In recent years it has become possible to see the United States in another way. Those who fly over it can see where the cities lie, and how much of the land they cover. They can see the patterns of the roads and rivers, the rise and fall of the land, its fertile and arid regions, and what they see is neither the changed

STATES IN THIS VOLUME

Alabama 24	Connecticut 44	Illinois 64	Maine 85
Alaska 27	Delaware 48	Indiana 68	Maryland 88
Arizona 30	Florida 50	Iowa 71	Massachusetts 91
Arkansas 33	Georgia 54	Kansas 74	Michigan 94
California 36	Hawaii 57	Kentucky 78	
Colorado 40	Idaho 60	Louisiana 82	

Introduction / 13

or the unchanged, but both. From east to west, the coast, the highlands, the plains, the mountains, the coast—region by region, in a few hours the United States can be seen from the air as nature made it and as man changed it.

The United States faces both the Atlantic and Pacific oceans, with the St. Lawrence River and the Great Lakes bringing ocean transportation almost to the center of the continent. Most of it lies in the middle latitudes. In Hawaii and Alaska, it has a share in tropical and Arctic regions.

It has almost every possible kind of land surface. Beginning at the Atlantic Ocean, there is a strip of lowland where settlers were able to gain a foothold in early colonial times. Farther inland, but nowhere more than a few hundred miles from the ocean, is the Appalachian Highland. Beyond the mountains is the Great Central Plain, the most productive farming area in the world. This plain extends from the Appalachians on the east to the Rockies on the west. Southward through this lowland flows the great Mississippi River, with tributaries reaching to the mountains on either side. The region is not flat. Most of it is rolling, with hilly areas here and there. West of the Mississippi River, it is interrupted by the Ozark Highlands, which resemble the Appalachians.

West of the Central Plain, again mountains rise. The wide Rocky Mountain System comes first. West of it is a region of high plains and plateaus, broken by short, low ranges of mountains and deeply cut by canyons. Still farther west are more mountains, the Sierras in the south and the Cascades in the north. Beyond them, actually dipping their feet in the Pacific Ocean, are the Coast Ranges.

Most of the highland West provides level land for farming only in the valleys, but no American would wish the highlands away. They are world-famous for their scenery, many of the slopes are heavily forested, and they are a great storehouse of valuable minerals.

The transformation of a large part of the North

Spacious Pennsylvania Avenue, parade route of Presidents, is in Washington, D.C., the capital of the United States.

REFERENCE MAPS

United States	14–15	Idaho	62–63
Alabama	24–25	Illinois	64–65
Alaska	28–29	Indiana	68–69
Arizona	30–31	Iowa	72–73
Arkansas	34–35	Kansas	74–75
California	36–37	Kentucky	80–81
Colorado	40–41	Louisiana	82–83
Connecticut	46–47	Maine	86–87
Delaware	49	Maryland	88–89
Florida	50–51	Massachusetts	92–93
Georgia	54–55	Michigan	94–95
Hawaii	58–59		

SPECIAL PURPOSE MAPS

United States-Physical Appearance	16–17
Population Map of the United States	19
United States Economy	20
Moisture Map of the United States	22

UNITED STATES

UNITED STATES

⊛ Capital

Washington, D.C. C11

Physical Features

Adirondack, mts	B12
Alabama, riv	D 9
Alaska, gulf	F 4
Alaska, pen	F 3
Alenuihaha, channel	F 6
Aleutian, is	F 3
Allegheny, mts	C10
Altamaha, riv	D10
Apalachee, bay	E10
Appalachian, mts	D 9
Arkansas, riv	C 8
Atchafalaya, bay	E 8
Baker, mtn	A 2
Baldy, peak	D 4
Bering, sea	F 3
Bering, strait	E 3
Big Horn, mts	B 5
Bighorn, riv	B 5
Bitterroot, range	A 3
Black, hills	B 6
Blue, mts	A 3
Blue Ridge, mts	D10
Boston, mts	C 8
Brazos, riv	D 7
Bristol, bay	F 3
Brooks, range	E 3
Canadian, riv	C 6
Cape Fear, riv	D11
Cascade, range	B 2
Charles, cape	C11
Chattahoochee, riv	D 9
Chesapeake, bay	C11
Chukchi, sea	E 3
Cimarron, riv	C 7
Coast, ranges	C 2
Cod, cape	B13
Colorado, plat	C 4
Colorado, riv	D 4
Colorado, riv	E 7
Columbia, riv	A 2
Conception, pt	D 2
Cumberland, isl	D10
Cumberland, riv	C 9
Death, val	C 3
Delaware, bay	C11
Des Moines, riv	B 8
Diamond Head, pt	F 5
Edwards, plat	D 6
Erie, lake	B10
Everglades, swamp	E10
Fear, cape	D11
Flattery, cape	A 1
Florida, bay	E10
Florida, straits	F10
Front, range	C 5
Garrison, res	A 6
Gila, riv	D 4
Granite, peak	A 5
Great, basin	C 3
Great Salt, lake	B 4
Great Smoky, mts	C 9
Green, mts	B12
Green, riv	C 5
Haleakala, crater	E 6
Hatteras, cape	C11
Hood, mtn	A 2
Hope, pt	E 3
Humboldt, riv	B 3
Huron, lake	B10
Illinois, riv	C 8
James, riv	A 7
James, riv	C11
Juan de Fuca, strait	A 1
Kaala, peak	F 5
Kaiwi, channel	E 6
Kansas, riv	C 7
Katahdin, mtn	A13
Kauai, channel	E 6
Kennedy, cape	E10
Kentucky, lake	C 9
Klamath, riv	B 2
Kodiak, isl	F 3
Kuskokwim, bay	F 3
Leech, lake	A 8

Lewis, range	A 4
Little Missouri, riv	A 6
Llano Estacado, plain	D 6
Lookout, cape	D11
McKinley, mtn	E 4
Marcy, mtn	B12
Matagorda, isl	E 7
May, cape	C13
Mead, lake	C 4
Mendocino, cape	B 1
Mexico, gulf	E 8
Michigan, lake	B 9
Milk, riv	A 5
Minnesota, riv	B 7
Mississippi, delta	E 9
Mississippi, riv	D 8
Missouri, riv	B 7
Mobile, bay	D 9
Mojave, des	C 3
Monterey, bay	C 2
Niobrara, riv	B 6
North Canadian, riv	C 6
North Platte, riv	B 5
Norton, sound	E 3
Nueces, riv	E 7
Oahe, res	A 7
Ohio, riv	C 9
Okeechobee, lake	E10
Ontario, lake	B11
Osage, riv	C 8
Ouachita, mts	D 8
Ouachita, riv	D 8
Ozark, plateau	C 8
Painted, des	C 4
Pamlico, sound	C11
Pearl, hbr	F 5
Pearl, riv	D 8
Pecos, riv	D 6
Pikes, peak	C 5
Platte, riv	B 6
Potomac, riv	C11
Powder, riv	A 5
Pyramid, lake	B 3
Red, lake	A 8
Red, riv	D 8
Red River, riv	A 7
Republican, riv	B 6
Rio Grande, riv	D 5
Roanoke, riv	C11
Rocky, mts	A 3
Romain, cape	D11
Romano, cape	E10
Romanzof, cape	E 3
Sabine, riv	D 8
Sable, cape	E10
Sacramento, mts	D 5
Sacramento, riv	C 2
St. Lawrence, riv	A13
Salmon River, mts	A 3
Salton, sea	D 3
San Blas, cape	E 9
San Clemente, isl	D 3
Sangre de Cristo, range	C 5
San Joaquin, riv	C 2
San Juan, riv	C 4
Santa Catalina, isl	D 3
Santa Rosa, isl	D 2
Santee, riv	D10
Savannah, riv	D10
Sevier, lake	C 4
Sevier, riv	C 4
Seward, pen	E 3
Sierra Nevada, mts	C 2
Snake, riv	B 3
Souris, riv	A 6
South Platte, riv	B 6
Superior, lake	A 9
Tahoe, lake	C 2
Tennessee, riv	D 9
Tombigbee, riv	D 9
Trinity, riv	D 7
Uinta, mts	B 4
Wabash, riv	C 9
Walker, lake	C 3
Wasatch, range	B 4
Washington, mtn	B12
Wheeler, peak	C 3
Whitney, mtn	C 3
Wisconsin, riv	B 8
Yellowstone, riv	A 5
Yukon, riv	E 3

Lambert Conformal Conic Projection
SCALE 1 : 15,217,000   1 Inch = 240 Statute Miles

The map represents land elevation by showing the landscape strongly lighted from the northwest. Highlights and shadows define the mountains and hills.

UNITED STATES

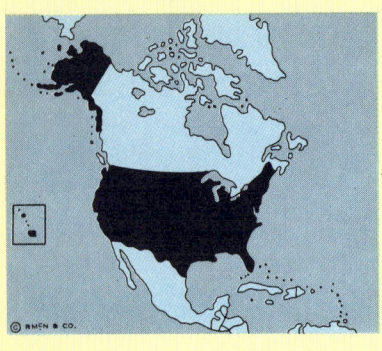

Capital: Washington, D. C.
Population (1970): 204,300,000
  Density: 56 per square mile
  Distribution: Urban: 73 per cent
         Rural: 27 per cent
Area: 3,675,547 square miles
Elevation: Highest point: 20,320 feet
       Lowest point: 282 feet below sea level

Principal language: English
Principal religions: Protestantism; Roman Catholicism
Political divisions: 50 states, 1 federal district
Currency unit: Dollar
National holiday: July 4, Independence Day
National anthem: Star Spangled Banner

American Continent into the United States of America began, in a sense, when the first small colonies were established on the Atlantic coast. Since that time, sometimes slowly, sometimes in great spurts, the people have moved westward; territory has been added, by purchase, by annexation, by treaty, until today the fifty states reach beyond the western border of the continent to Hawaii.

In 1776, the people of the thirteen British colonies declared themselves independent. They created a new nation, which they called the United States of America.

At the end of the War for Independence, the treaty of 1783 made the Mississippi River the western boundary of the new United States. Florida, with southern Alabama and Mississippi, was not included, nor was Louisiana.

Until this time the Appalachian Mountains had been the backstop for settlement. In 1783, only a few settlers lived on the wide plain between the Appalachians and the Mississippi. It was believed then that settlement of this region might take 100 years, but within a few years settlers began pouring in. In 1803, President Jefferson bought Louisiana for the United States. The Louisiana Purchase included all the land

Steep-sided cliffs cast their shadows in the chasms of Arizona's Grand Canyon, a monument to time carved by the Colorado River.

POPULATION MAP

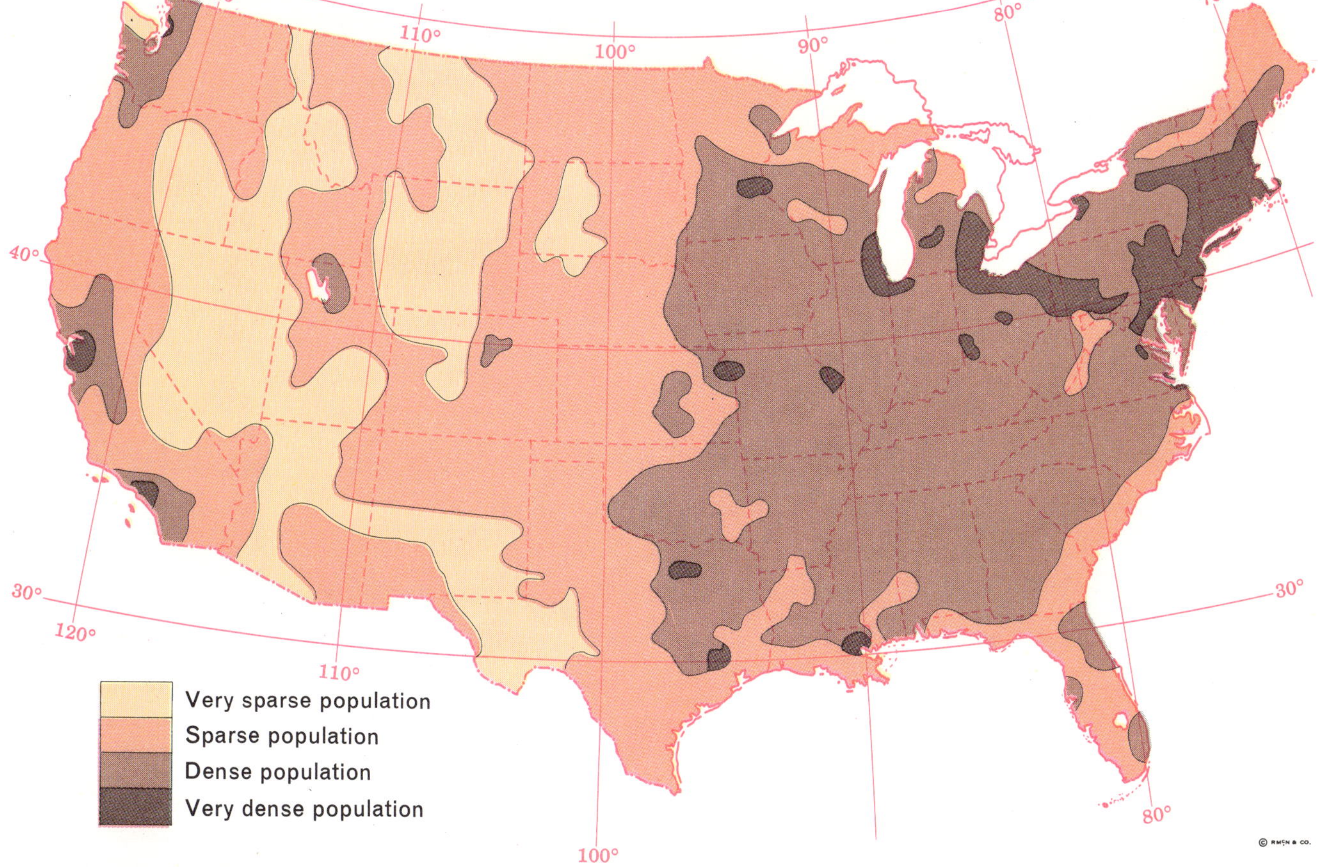

- Very sparse population
- Sparse population
- Dense population
- Very dense population

Midday in the renowned financial district of New York City

20 / TODAY'S WORLD

UNITED STATES
ECONOMY

ECONOMY

HEAVY INDUSTRY
- Machinery
- Metal Processing
- Metal Processing Iron
- Metal Processing Steel
- Metal Processing Aluminum
- Petroleum Refining
- Transportation Equipment Aircraft
- Transportation Equipment Automobiles
- Transportation Equipment Railroad
- Transportation Equipment Ship

LIGHT INDUSTRY
- Electrical & Electronic Products
- Chemicals
- Clothing
- Dairy Products
- Food Processing
- Furniture
- Leather Products
- Lumber & Forest Products
- Building Materials
- Metal Products

OTHERS
- Fishing
- Seaport
- Tourists & Resorts
- Water Power
- Printing & Publishing
- Motion Pictures
- Pulp & Paper Products
- Rubber Products
- Stone Clay & Glass Products
- Textiles
- Textiles & Clothing
- Insurance
- Atomic Power
- Fishing Areas

MINING
- B Bauxite
- Ce Cement
- Cl Clay
- C Coal
- Cu Copper
- G Gold
- I Iron Ore
- L Lead
- Li Lignite
- Mr Mercury
- Mo Molybdenum
- Gs Natural Gas
- Pm Petroleum
- P Phosphate
- Pl Platinum
- Po Potash
- SG Sand & Gravel
- S Silver
- St Stone
- Su Sulphur
- Tu Tungsten
- U Uranium
- Va Vanadium
- Z Zinc

AGRICULTURE
- General Farming
- Feed Grains & Livestock
- Wheat & Small Grains
- Cotton
- Special Crops & General Farming
- Special Crops & General Farming (Irrigated)
- Fruit, Truck & General Farming
- Fruit, Truck & General Farming (Irrigated)
- Sugar Cane
- Dairy & General Farming
- Year Long Grazing
- Seasonal Grazing
- Desert
- Swamp Land
- Forests

drained by rivers flowing toward the Mississippi on its western side. Thus in one year the United States expanded to twice its original size.

Less than 20 years later, Florida was added to the United States by a treaty with Spain. In 1836, Texans declared themselves independent of Mexico, and ten years later joined the United States. Disputes over the Texas boundary led to a war with Mexico. As a result of this war, the United States annexed the old Spanish lands all the way to the Pacific Ocean, except for a small section of Arizona and New Mexico, which was later bought from Mexico. Until 1846, no northern boundary had been drawn west of the Rockies. The land was occupied jointly by the United States and Britain, since both had good claims. In 1846, the "Oregon Question" was settled by agreement. The forty-ninth parallel became the boundary, and is still the boundary between the United States and Canada.

By 1853, the main area of the United States had reached its present size. The country took its first step beyond the Pacific coast in 1867. In that year Secretary of State Seward negotiated with Russia for the purchase of Alaska. This transaction turned out to be one of the best bargains the United States ever made.

Almost to the end of the nineteenth century, Hawaii was an independent country. In 1898, the United States annexed the islands. With this annexation all the land in the present fifty states had been acquired, though some of the areas were still territories and did not become states until later.

While the United States was growing in area, it was also growing in population. From a beginning with fewer than 5,000,000 people, the population had grown to 90,000,000 when Hawaii was annexed. By the time Hawaii became a state sixty-two years later, the population of the United States had doubled again.

The densest population is still, as it was in the beginning, in the eastern half of the continental states,

Chimneys and fractionating towers rise among the storage tanks and buildings of an oil refinery in Tulsa, Oklahoma.

22 / TODAY'S WORLD

MOISTURE MAP

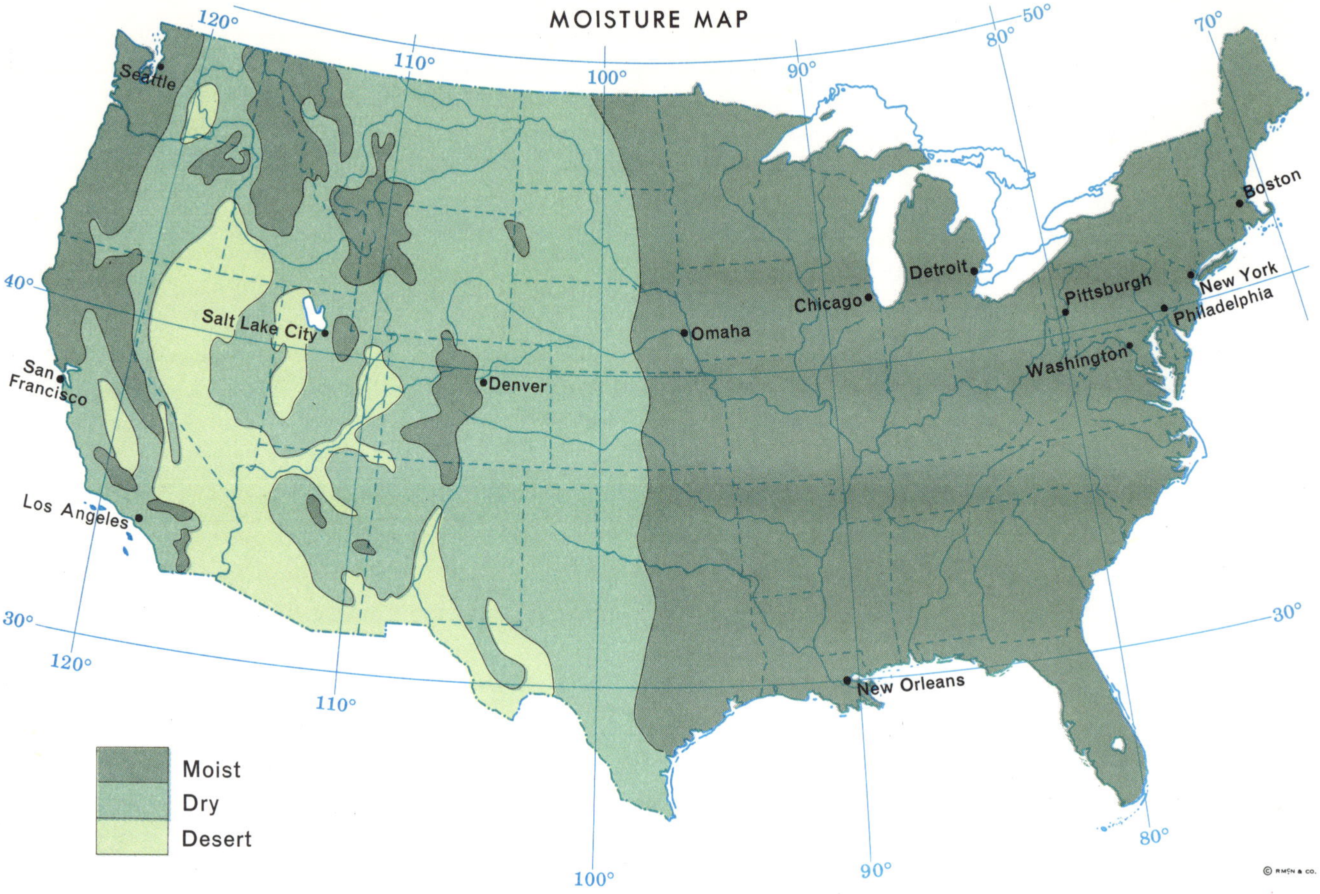

- Moist
- Dry
- Desert

Spiked with rocks and spotted with brush growth, the western deserts reach to the horizon tinted by ever-changing colors.

A country road curves through a quiet, rural scene in mountainous southeastern Idaho, near Bear Lake.

with smaller patches of dense population along the Pacific coast. Elsewhere the population of the West is sparse.

Most of the land between the Rockies on the east and the Sierras and Cascades on the west is true desert, too dry to support any kind of farming without irrigation. Very little is entirely without vegetation. In the north, the gray-green of sagebrush colors many square miles. In the south, cactus plants flame into brilliant bloom in the spring. Creosote bushes are covered with yellow blossoms, and the delicate agave flowers rise above their sword-shaped leaves.

In spite of its great agricultural regions, only about 4 per cent of the employed people in the United States are farmers. The other 96 per cent are employed in other occupations. Indirectly, however, they still depend upon the productivity of the land; they must have food. Also thousands upon thousands of people work in factories that process farm products, and in these days of mechanized farming, thousands more work in factories that make farm machines and equipment and transportation equipment. Others work in stores, or teach, practice law or medicine, or work in a complex of industries. Industry in the United States is even more diverse than the land itself.

Among all the fifty states, no two are exactly alike. Each has its reasons for pride in its accomplishments, each has its own assortment of resources, and each has made its contributions to the growth and prosperity of the country.

ALABAMA

ALABAMA
Principal Cities
Pop.—Thousands

Pop	City	Ref
3	Abbeville	D 4
2	Adamsville	f 7
2	Alabaster	B 3
8	Albertville	A 3
13	Alexander City	C 4
3	Aliceville	B 1
10	Andalusia	D 3
34	Anniston	B 4
3	Arab	A 3
2	Ashford	D 4
2	Ashland	B 4
14	Athens	A 3
8	Atmore	D 2
8	Attalla	A 3
16	Auburn	C 4
5	Bay Minette	E 2
3	Bayou La Batre	E 1
33	Bessemer	B 3, g 7
341	Birmingham	B 3, f 7
4	Bluff Park	g 7
5	Boaz	A 3
1	Boylston	C 3
1	Brantley	C 3
2	Brent	C 2
6	Brewton	D 2
3	Bridgeport	A 4
3	Brighton	B 3, g 7
3	Brundidge	D 4
2	Butler	C 1
5	Cahaba Heights	B 3
2	Calera	B 3
1	Camden	D 2
1	Camp Hill	C 4
2	Carbon Hill	B 2
15	Center Point	f 7
2	Centre	A 4
2	Centreville	C 2
1	Cherokee	A 2
10	Chickasaw	E 1
5	Childersburg	B 3
2	Citronelle	D 1
6	Clanton	C 3
1	Clayton	D 4
1	Coden	E 1
2	Columbiana	B 3
3	Cordova	B 2
11	Cullman	A 3
3	Dadeville	C 4
3	Daleville	D 4
2	Daphne	E 2
29	Decatur	A 3
7	Demopolis	C 2
3	Dolomite	B 3, g 7
2	Dora	B 2
31	Dothan	D 4
3	East Brewton	D 2
4	Elba	D 3
11	Enterprise	D 4
8	Eufaula	D 4
3	Eutaw	C 2
4	Evergreen	D 3
3	Fairfax	C 4
16	Fairfield	B 3, g 7
5	Fairfield Highlands	B 3
5	Fairhope	E 2
4	Fayette	B 2
1	Flomaton	D 2
3	Florala	D 3
32	Florence	A 2
3	Foley	E 2
1	Fort Deposit	D 3
1	Fort Payne	A 7
1	Frisco City	D 2
3	Fultondale	f 7
58	Gadsden	A 4
6	Gardendale	B 3, f 7
4	Geneva	D 4
2	Georgiana	D 3
3	Glencoe	B 4
2	Goodwater	B 3
2	Gordo	B 2
3	Graysville	f 7
3	Greensboro	C 2
7	Greenville	D 3
2	Grove Hill	D 2
7	Guntersville	A 3
4	Haleyville	A 2

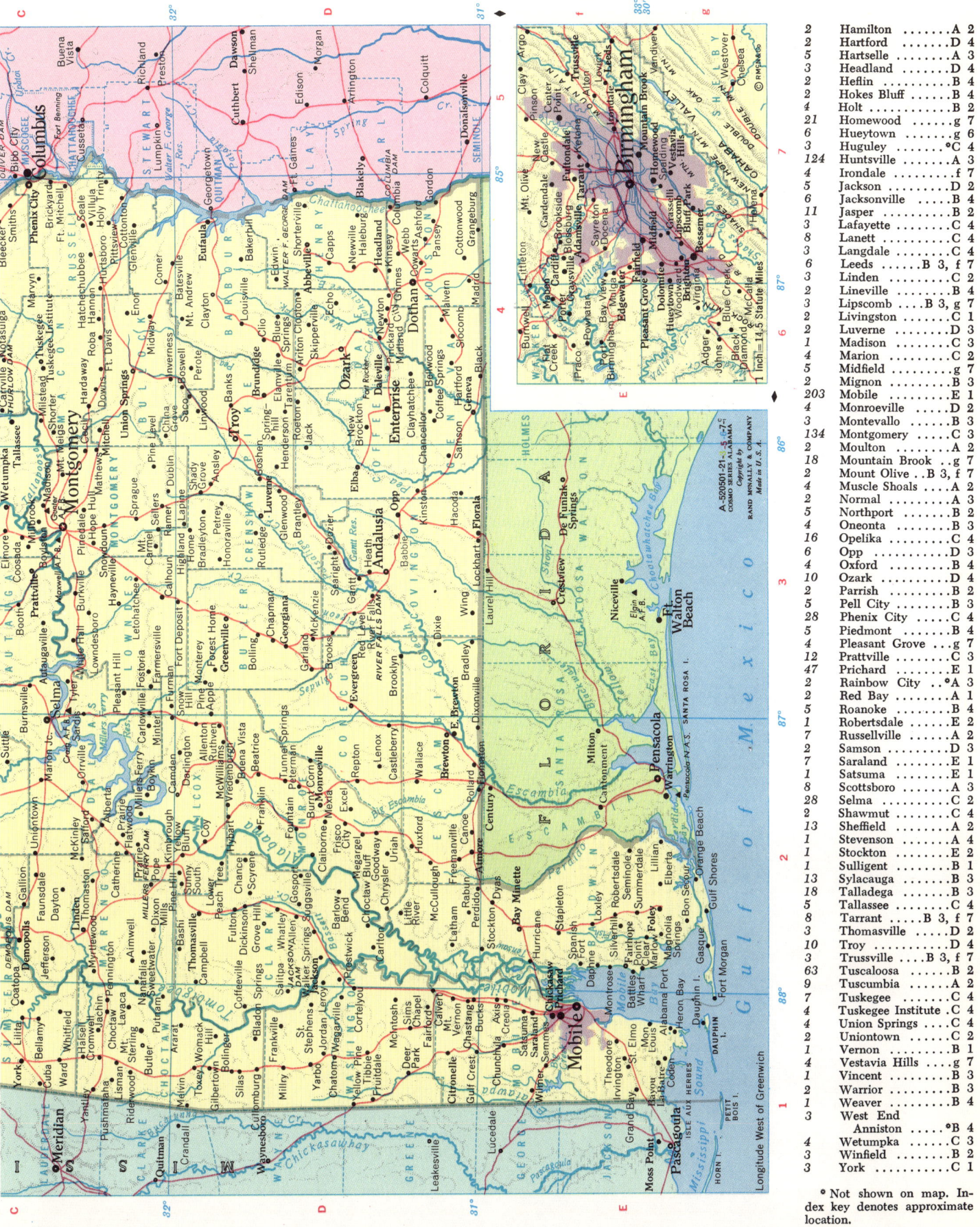

ALABAMA

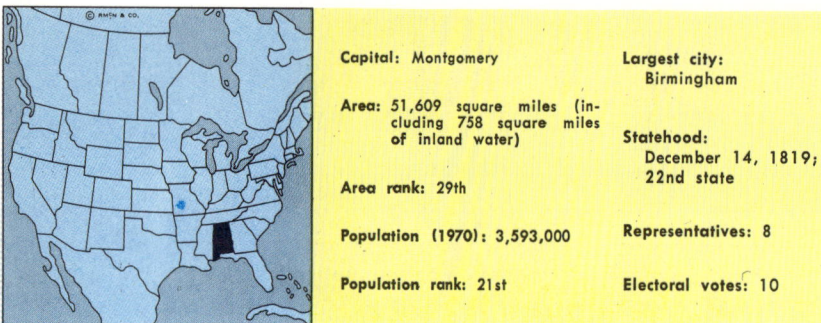

Capital: Montgomery

Area: 51,609 square miles (including 758 square miles of inland water)

Area rank: 29th

Population (1970): 3,593,000

Population rank: 21st

Largest city: Birmingham

Statehood: December 14, 1819; 22nd state

Representatives: 8

Electoral votes: 10

Alabama lies halfway between the Atlantic Ocean and the Mississippi River. Mobile, its port on the Gulf of Mexico, trades with Latin America to the south, but its greatest industrial regions are in the north. Traditionally agricultural, Alabama is still a state of productive farms, with pasture for cattle replacing some of the former cotton fields. It has two main centers of industrial development, one based on the iron and steel industry around Birmingham and the other on the power resources of the Tennessee Valley. There are three TVA dams in the state.

Alabama's climate is favorable for agriculture; warm, with fifty to sixty inches of annual rainfall over most of the state. Usually enough rain falls in July when the crops need it most.

The French came in 1699 to Mobile, a fine natural harbor at a river mouth, but they did little to extend settlement in Alabama. It was settlers moving overland from the Atlantic coastal regions who peopled the interior. Alabama became an organized territory in 1817, a state two years later. Montgomery, the thriving capital city, was in 1861 the first capital of the Confederacy.

Alabama's development followed the pattern of other Cotton Belt states. First came cattlemen with their herds and then farmers who practiced mixed farming. Later cotton growers moved in. Montgomery and Mobile grew prosperous in trade. Then came the disruption of the Civil War. Most farmers continued to grow cotton for many years, but later many shifted to cattle or to growing specialty crops. As in the other southern states, turpentine and lumber from the forests provided additional revenue.

One development came as a by-product of the Civil War. To make cannon balls, men had used the iron ore, limestone, and coal that were found at Red Mountain. In 1871, Birmingham was established there and, with it, Alabama's iron-and-steel industry.

Alabama's second opportunity for industrialization came after 1935, when the Tennessee Valley Authority (TVA) began harnessing the Tennessee River with a chain of dams and powerhouses. Cheap electric power attracted metal industries to Florence, Decatur, and Sheffield. Cotton mills, food-processing plants, and other industries are scattered over the state.

The most important industry in Alabama is iron and steel manufacturing. Most of the plants are in or near Birmingham.

The bold, snow-clad peaks and massive glacier of the Alaskan mountains

ALASKA

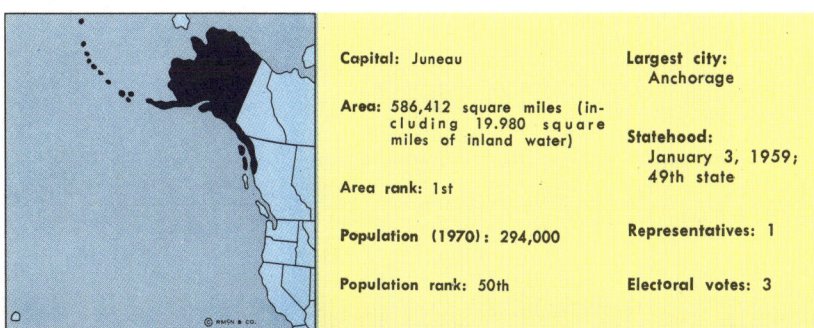

Capital: Juneau

Area: 586,412 square miles (including 19,980 square miles of inland water)

Area rank: 1st

Population (1970): 294,000

Population rank: 50th

Largest city: Anchorage

Statehood: January 3, 1959; 49th state

Representatives: 1

Electoral votes: 3

Alaska, the forty-ninth state, is by far the largest in the Union. It occupies the northwest extremity of North America. Most of the state is a large peninsula, but it also includes a narrow strip of land extending far southward along the Pacific coast. A narrow finger of land reaches west, continued by a chain of islands called the Aleutians.

Alaska boasts the highest mountain on the North American continent, Mount McKinley. The state contains more wildlife than any other state, and it has the smallest population. Less than one-sixth of the people are Eskimos, Aleuts, and Indians.

Far from being an arctic waste, most of it is forested and there are industries based on wood. Successful farming operations are carried on, and there is an agricultural experiment station as far north as Fairbanks. Warmed by Pacific winds, southeastern Alaska compares in climate with the Pacific coast of Washington and Oregon. In the interior, temperatures vary from almost 100 degrees in summer to 66 degrees below zero in winter.

Alaskan salmon fisheries are the largest in the world. Timber, fur, and mineral deposits also add to the economy. In 1968, the great oil discovery at Prudhoe Bay, on the north slope of Brooks Range, enriched the economy beyond belief. The area will be one of the world's biggest producers.

Alaska's largest city is Anchorage, a port and a stopping place for planes flying between the United States and eastern Asia. Alaska's best farmland, the Matanuska Valley, is near Anchorage. From Anchorage, Alaska's only long railway runs north to Fairbanks. Alaska's capital and fourth largest city is Juneau.

In the mid-eighteenth century Russian traders appeared in Alaska, and trading posts were built. The Aleuts, who hunted and trapped for the Russians, traveled as far south as San Francisco.

The United States did not take kindly to the Russian activities in California. The Monroe Doctrine, announced in 1823, had the Russians very much in view. Fortunately Alaska became less attractive to the czars, and the United States purchased it in 1867.

ALASKA

Principal Cities

Pop.—Thousands		
45	Anchorage	C10, g17
1	Barrow	A 8
1	Bethel	C 7
3	College	C10
1	Cordova	C10, g19
1	Douglas	D13, k22
1	Eagle River	g16
13	Fairbanks	C10
2	Hamilton Acres	*C 7
1	Homer	D 9, h16
7	Juneau	D13, k22
6	Ketchikan	D13, n24
3	Kodiak	D 9
1	Kotzebue	B 7
1	Lemeta	*C10
2	Mount Edgecumbe	m22
2	Nome	C 6
2	Nunaka Valley	g17
1	Palmer	C10, g17
2	Petersburg	D13, m23
2	Seward	C10, g17
3	Sitka	D12, m22
12	Spenard	g16
1	Wrangell	D13, m23

Pop.—Hundreds		
2	Akiachak	C 7
2	Akiak	C 7
1	Akutan	E 6
3	Alakanuk	C 7
2	Aleknagik	D 8
1	Allakaket	B 9
2	Anchor Point	D 9, h16
4	Angoon	D13, m22
3	Aniak	C 8
4	Annette	n24
1	Anvik	C 7
1	Arctic Village	B10
1	Atka	E 5
5	Auke Bay	k22
1	Beaver	B10
1	Belkofski	D 7
1	Bettles Field	B 9
1	Big Delta	C10
1	Buckland	B 7
4	Carlana	n24
1	Chefornak	*C 7
3	Chevak	*C 7
1	Chignik	D 8
9	Chugiak	C10, g17
1	Clarks Point	D 8
1	Cold Bay	*E 7
2	Copper Center	C10, g19
3	Craig	D13, n23
1	Crooked Creek	C 8
1	Deering	B 7
3	Delta Junction	*C10
4	Dillingham	D 8
1	Diomede	*B 6
1	Edna Bay	m23
2	Eek	C 7
2	Egegik	D 8
1	Ekwak	D 8
1	Elim	C 7
1	Excursion Inlet	k22
7	Fort Yukon	B10
3	Galena	C 8
4	Gambell	C 5
2	Glennallen	f19
2	Goodnews Bay	D 7
4	Haines	D12, k22
3	Holy Cross	C 8
7	Hoonah	D12, k22
5	Hooper Bay	C 6
2	Huslia	*B 8
3	Hydaburg	D13, n23
5	Kake	D13, m23
1	Kalskag	C 7
2	Kaltag	C 8
1	Karluk	D 9
2	Kasigluk	*C 7
8	Kenai	C 9, g16
3	Kiana	B 7
3	King Cove	D 7
2	Kipnuk	C 7

1	Kivalina	B 7
3	Klawock	D13, n23
1	Klukwan	k22
1	Koyuk	C 7
1	Koyukuk	C 8
3	Kwethluk	°C 7
1	Kwigillingok	D 7
4	Kwiguk	C 7
1	Lower Kalskag	°C 7
2	McGrath	C 8
1	Manley Hot Springs	B 9
1	Manokotak	D 8
2	Mekoryuk	C 6
8	Metlakatla	D13, n14
2	Minto	C10
1	Moose Pass	C10, g17
4	Mountain Point	n22
1	Mountain Village	C 7
2	Naknek	D 8
2	Napakiak	C 7
3	Nenana	C10
1	New Stuyahok	°D 8
2	Ninilchik	C 9, g16
3	Noatak	B 7
2	Nondalton	C 8
4	Noorvik	B 7
6	North Pole	°C10
1	Northway	°C11
2	Nulato	C 8
3	Nunapitchuk	°C 7
2	Nyac	C 8
2	Old Harbor	D 9
2	Ouzinkie	D 9
1	Pelican	k21
1	Perryville	D 8
2	Pilot Station	C 7
3	Point Hope	B 6
1	Port Chilkoot	D12, k22
1	Port Graham	D 9, h16
2	Quinhagak	D 7
2	Ruby	C 8
3	St. George	°D 6
2	St. Marys	°C 7
2	St. Michael	C 7
4	St. Paul	°D 8
2	Sand Point	D 7
3	Savoonga	C 5
1	Scammon Bay	C 6
4	Selawik	B 7
5	Seldovia	D 9, h16
2	Shageluk	C 8
2	Shaktoolik	C 7
2	Sheldon Point	°C 7
1	Shishmaref	B 6
2	Shungnak	B 8
7	Skagway	D12, k22
2	Sleetmute	C 8
1	South Naknek	D 8
2	Stebbins	C 7
2	Suntrana	C10
1	Sutton	g17
2	Talkeetna	C 9, f16
3	Tanacross	C11
1	Tanana	B 9
3	Tatitlek	C10, g18
2	Teller	B 6
1	Tenakee Springs	D12, m22
2	Togiak	D 7
2	Tok	°C11
1	Tuluksak	°C 7
1	Tuntatuliak	C 7
2	Tyonek	C 9, g16
6	Unalakleet	C 7
1	Unalaska	E 6
6	Valdez	C10, g18
1	Venetie	B10
1	Wainwright	A 7
1	Wales	B 6
1	Wasilla	C10, g17
2	White Mountain	C 7
7	Whittier	C10, g17
2	Yakutat	D12

° Not shown on map. Index key denotes approximate location.

ARIZONA

ARIZONA
Principal Cities
Pop.—Thousands

Pop	City	Grid
7	Ajo	E 3
3	Apache Junction	m 9
7	Avondale	m 8
2	Bagdad	C 2
2	Benson	F 5
10	Bisbee	F 6
2	Buckeye	D 3, m 7
1	Buckhorn	D 4, m 9
1	Bullhead City	B 1
8	Casa Grande	E 4
5	Casas Adobes	°E 5
1	Cashion	D 3
1	Cave Creek	D 4, k 9
2	Central Heights	D 5
12	Chandler	D 4, m 9
1	Clarkdale	C 3
2	Claypool	D 5
4	Clifton	D 6
5	Coolidge	E 4
2	Cottonwood	C 3
12	Douglas	F 6
1	Eagar	C 6
3	El Mirage	k 8
5	Eloy	E 4
25	Flagstaff	B 4
2	Florence	D 4
2	Gila Bend	E 3
2	Gilbert	D 4, m 9
31	Glendale	D 3, k 8
6	Globe	D 5
2	Goodyear	D 3, m 8
2	Guadalupe	m 9
2	Hayden	E 5
4	Holbrook	C 5
1	Huachuca City	F 5
2	Kearney	D 5
6	Kingman	B 1
2	Litchfield Park	m 8
2	McNary	C 6
2	Mammoth	E 5
51	Mesa	D 4, m 9
3	Miami	D 5
2	Morenci	D 6
7	Nogales	F 5
1	Oracle	E 5
3	Page	A 4
5	Paradise Valley	m 9
2	Parker	C 1
1	Payson	C 4
4	Peoria	D 3, k 8
506	Phoenix	D 3, m 8
1	Pima	E 6
2	Plantsite	D 6
14	Prescott	C 3
1	Ray	D 5
5	Safford	E 6
1	St. Johns	C 6
5	San Manuel	E 5
55	Scottsdale	D 4, m 9
5	Show Low	C 5
5	Sierra Vista	F 5
2	Snowflake	C 5
2	Somerton	E 1
7	South Tucson	E 5
1	Springerville	C 6
1	Stargo	D 6
5	Superior	D 4
2	Surprise	k 8
46	Tempe	D 4, m 9
2	Thatcher	E 6
4	Tolleson	m 8
1	Tombstone	F 5
237	Tucson	E 5
1	Valencia	m 7
3	West Yuma	°E 1
2	Wickenburg	D 3
2	Willcox	E 6
4	Williams	B 3
1	Winkelman	E 5
9	Winslow	C 5
2	Youngtown	k 8
28	Yuma	E 1

Pop.—Hundreds

Pop	City	Grid
3	Aguila	D 2
3	Alpine	D 6
8	Ash Fork	B 3
4	Black Canyon City	C 3

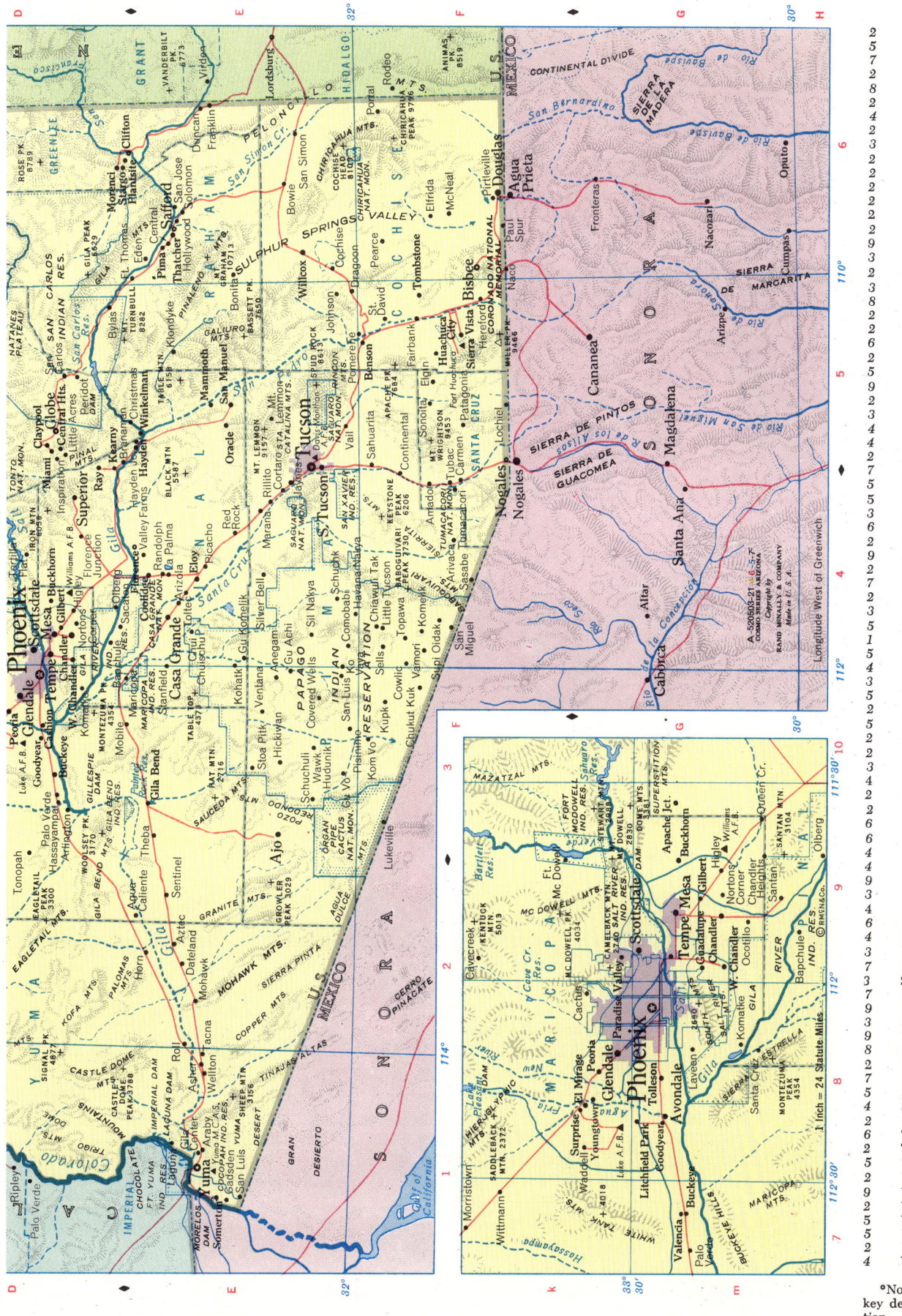

2	Bouse	D 2
5	Bowie	E 6
7	Bullhead City	B 1
2	Bylas	D 5
8	Camp Verde	C 4
2	Chambers	B 6
4	Chandler Heights	m 9
2	Chinle	A 6
3	Chino Valley	C 3
2	Christmas	F 5
3	Clay Springs	C 5
2	Concho	C 6
2	Congress	C 3
2	Cornfield	B 6
2	Davis Dam	B 1
9	Duncan	E 6
3	Ehrenberg	D 1
2	Elfrida	F 6
3	Forbing Park	C 3
8	Fort Defiance	B 6
2	Fort McDowell	k 9
5	Fort Thomas	D 6
2	Fredonia	A 3
5	Gadsden	E 1
2	Ganado	B 6
9	Grand Canyon	A 3
2	Groom Creek	C 3
3	Gu Achi	E 3
4	Happy Jack	C 4
4	Heber	C 5
2	Hereford	F 5
7	Hotevilla	A 4
5	Humboldt	C 3
5	Inspiration	D 5
3	Jaynes	E 4
6	Joseph City	C 5
2	Kayenta	A 5
9	Keams Canyon	B 5
3	Klagetoh	B 6
7	Lakeside	C 6
2	Laveen	m 8
4	Little Acres	D 5
5	Lower Miami	°D 5
1	Lupton	B 6
5	Marana	E 4
3	Maricopa	E 3
4	Mayer	C 3
5	Moenkopi	A 4
2	Morristown	D 3, k 7
2	Naco	F 6
9	Nutrioso	D 6
2	Ocotillo	m 9
5	Olberg	D 4, m 9
2	Oraibi	B 5
6	Overgaard	C 5
2	Palo Verde	D 3, m 7
6	Patagonia	F 5
6	Peach Springs	B 2
2	Picacho	E 4
4	Pinetop	C 6
4	Pirtleville	F 6
5	Polacca	B 5
2	Quartzsite	D 1
4	Queen Creek	m 9
9	Randolph	E 4
3	Rillito	E 4
2	Sacaton	D 4
7	Sahuarita	F 5
7	St. David	F 5
4	San Carlos	D 5
3	Sanders	B 6
8	Seligman	B 3
9	Sells	F 4
2	Show Low	C 5
7	Silver Bell	E 4
8	Solomon	E 6
4	Stanfield	E 3
5	Tanque Verde	°F 5
6	Taylor	C 5
5	Topawa	F 4
2	Tuba City	A 4
6	Valley Farms	E 4
9	Wellton	E 1
2	Wenden	D 2
5	Whiteriver	D 6
5	Window Rock	B 6
5	Wittmann	D 3, k 7
4	Yarnell	C 3

°Not shown on map. Index key denotes approximate location.

In today's mechanized world, cowhands still keep herds of white-faced herefords on the move at round-up time.

ARIZONA

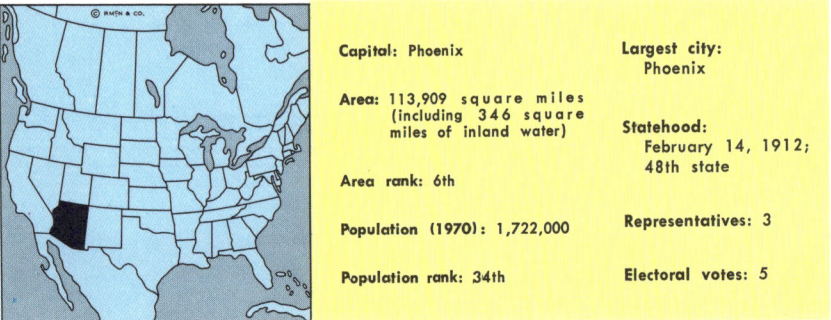

Capital: Phoenix

Area: 113,909 square miles (including 346 square miles of inland water)

Area rank: 6th

Population (1970): 1,722,000

Population rank: 34th

Largest city: Phoenix

Statehood: February 14, 1912; 48th state

Representatives: 3

Electoral votes: 5

All of Arizona lies within the Intermountain region, the driest part of the United States. In the south and west of the state is true desert, where the giant saguaro cactus, which may be 50 feet in height and weigh ten tons, and many other desert plants grow. This land cannot be farmed, except where it can be irrigated, and most of it cannot even be used for grazing. Winters are dry, mild, almost cloudless. Summer temperatures regularly exceed 100 degrees, but low humidity and a 30-degree drop at night make them tolerable.

A mountain region crosses the state from Lake Mead to the headwaters of the Gila River. There are stands of pine and aspen and cattle ranches in this area, and the highest mountain has a ski center.

The northern and northeastern two-thirds of the state, made up of mountains and plateaus, are almost as dry but less hot because the land is higher, rising in places to more than 7,000 feet. Most of this higher region is used for grazing. The Colorado River has cut through this northern plateau region to make the Grand Canyon, a gash a mile deep in places and about 200 miles long, where more than 500,000,000 years of the earth's history are revealed in spectacular layers of colored rock.

The Navajo Indian Reservation, including dramatic Monument Valley, covers much of northern Arizona. Many of the Navajos still lead a nomadic life, following their herds from summer to winter range, but changes are coming. Highways are being built across the reservation and pickup trucks are almost as common as horse-drawn wagons. The small Hopi Reservation, with its ancient towns perched on the edge of high, narrow mesas, lies within the Navajo reservation.

In the sixteenth and seventeenth centuries explorers and missionaries came into Arizona from the south and claimed the territory for Spain. The new Mexican republic took over in 1822. Through the Mexican War (1848) and Gadsden Purchase (1853), Arizona became United States territory. Mining towns and the cattle boom brought in rough-and-ready settlers, and towns, like notorious Tombstone, grew to the sound of the saloon piano and the six-shooter. The Theodore Roosevelt era brought modern irrigation and farming. In 1912, Arizona was granted statehood.

ARKANSAS

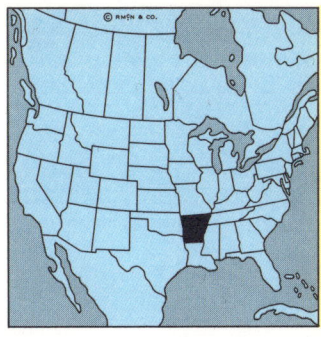

Capital: Little Rock	**Largest city:** Little Rock
Area: 53,104 square miles (including 929 square miles of inland water)	**Statehood:** June 15, 1836; 25th state
Area rank: 27th	
Population (1970): 2,006,000	**Representatives:** 4
Population rank: 32nd	**Electoral votes:** 6

Arkansas has a variety of natural resources. The state's inhabitants include farmers, lumbermen, factory workers, river boatmen, railroaders, miners, and resort operators.

The state is a place of long, hot summers and short and fairly cold winters. Rainfall is from 30 to 40 inches and is well distributed through the year.

Arkansas can be divided into four sections. The flat, fertile belt that forms the eastern quarter of the state is the Mississippi River bottoms. On rich alluvial soil here are the farms that make Arkansas the fourth largest cotton producer in the nation. Soybeans and rice are also important products.

The Ozark Plateau occupies most of the northern part of the state and extends into Missouri. The low Boston and Ouachita mountains roughen the surface of northwestern Arkansas. The highlands are clothed with hardwood forests, and there are some general farming regions.

The fourth type of land in Arkansas is made up of its valleys. Next to the Mississippi Valley, the valley of the Arkansas River is the most important. This river flows through the middle of the state, separating the two upland regions. The valley land is fertile, producing a share of the cotton and various specialty crops. The valley is also a principal communications artery. It is a main route for rail and highway traffic, and Arkansas's three largest urban centers—Little Rock, Fort Smith, and Pine Bluff—are located on this river.

Southern Arkansas has oil and gas fields, which are the basis for an eighty-million-dollar industry. Arkansas mines bauxite, barite (a barium sulfate ore), and bromine; it also has deposits of coal.

The forests supply the raw material for the principal industries of the state. Sawmills, paper mills, and furniture factories are widely distributed over the state. There are forests, not only in the highlands, but along the Mississippi and in the south.

Arkansas's special endowments give it a substantial tourist trade. The highlands constitute one of the mid-continent's great recreation areas for hunting, fishing, and camping. A number of dams have created large lakes, and the natural mineral springs, known to the Indians as "cures" before the settlers came, are popular attractions.

Rice is raised in eastern Arkansas with modern efficiency. Here a pair of combines are harvesting the ripened grain.

ARKANSAS

ARKANSAS
Principal Cities
Pop.—Thousands

Pop	City	Ref
2	Alma	B 1
1	Altheimer	C 4
10	Arkadelphia	C 2
3	Ashdown	D 1
1	Atkins	B 3
3	Augusta	B 4
2	Bald Knob	B 4
1	Barling	B 1
7	Batesville	B 4
1	Bearden	D 3
2	Beebe	B 4
16	Benton	C 3, k 9
5	Bentonville	A 1
2	Berryville	A 2
26	Blytheville	B 6
3	Booneville	B 2
5	Brinkley	C 4
1	Bryant	C 3, k 9
2	Cabot	C 3
15	Camden	D 3
1	Cammack Village	C 3, h10
1	Caraway	B 5
2	Carlisle	C 4
1	Charleston	B 1
3	Clarendon	C 4
4	Clarksville	B 2
1	Clinton	B 3
15	Conway	B 3
3	Corning	A 5
2	Cotton Plant	B 4
6	Crossett	D 4
1	Danville	B 2
3	Dardanelle	B 2
4	De Queen	C 1
4	McDermott	D 4
2	Des Arc	C 4
4	De Witt	C 4
1	Dierks	C 1
4	Dumas	D 4
3	Earle	B 5
26	El Dorado	D 3
3	England	C 4, k11
4	Eudora	D 4
2	Eureka Springs	A 2
30	Fayetteville	A 1
5	Fordyce	D 3
1	Foreman	D 1
13	Forrest City	B 5
64	Fort Smith	B 1
3	Genevia	C 3, k10
2	Glenwood	C 2
2	Gould	D 4
1	Gravette	A 1
1	Green Forrest	A 2
2	Greenwood	B 1
2	Gurdon	D 2
3	Hamburg	D 4
1	Hampton	D 3
5	Harrisburg	B 5
7	Harrison	A 2
1	Hazen	C 4
2	Heber Springs	B 3
12	Helena	C 5
8	Hope	D 2
29	Hot Springs	C 2, f 7
2	Hoxie	A 5
1	Huntsville	A 2
18	Jacksonville	C 3, h10
27	Jonesboro	B 5
1	Jones Mill	C 3, g 8
1	Judsonia	B 4
3	Lake Village	D 4
2	Leachville	B 5
2	Lepanto	B 5
2	Lewisville	D 2
129	Little Rock	C 3, k10
3	Lonoke	C 4, h11
1	Luxora	B 6
1	McCrory	B 4
4	McGehee	D 4
11	Magnolia	D 2
9	Malvern	C 3, g 8
1	Mammoth Spring	A 4
2	Manila	B 5
6	Marianna	C 5
3	Marked Tree	B 5

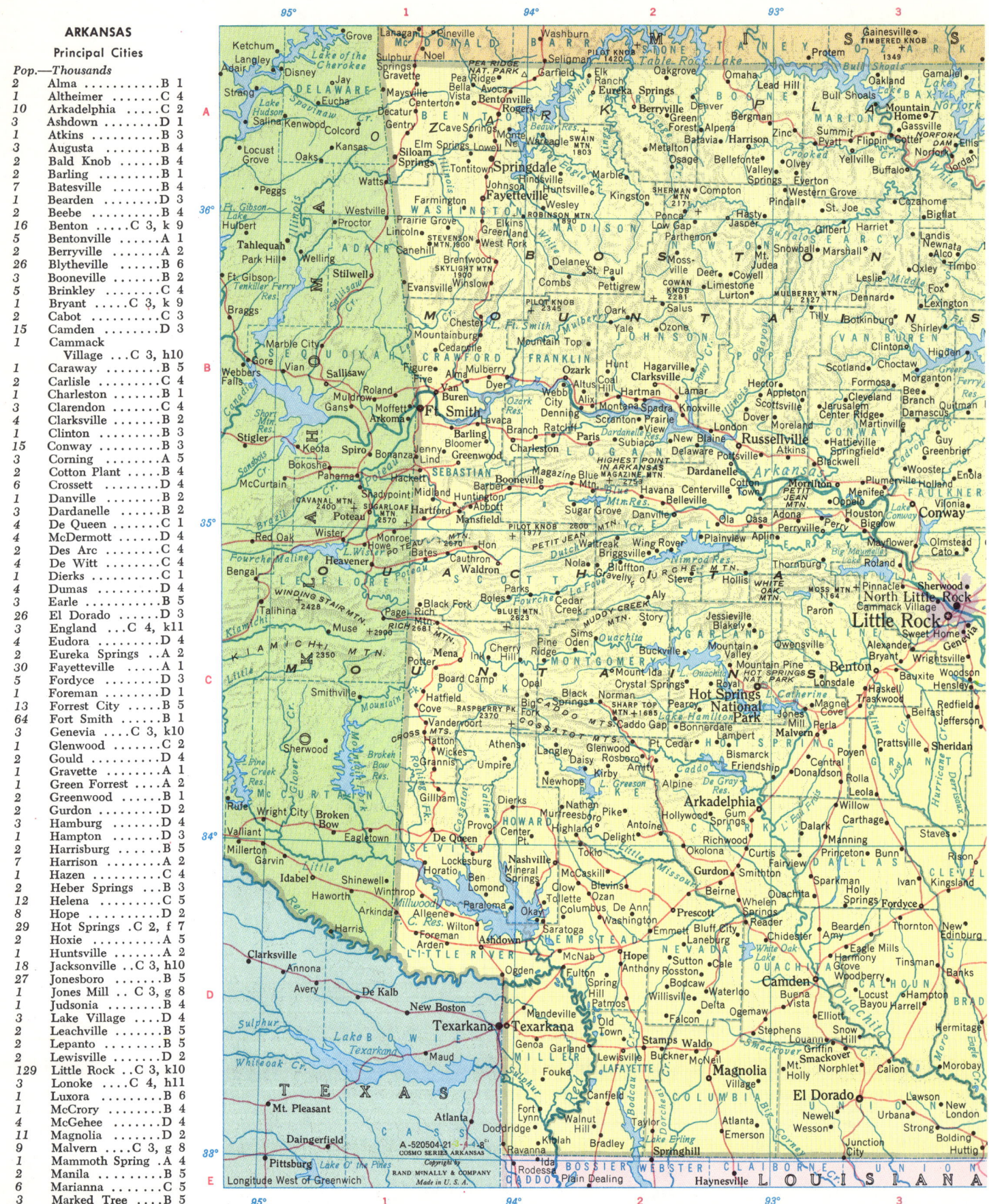

35

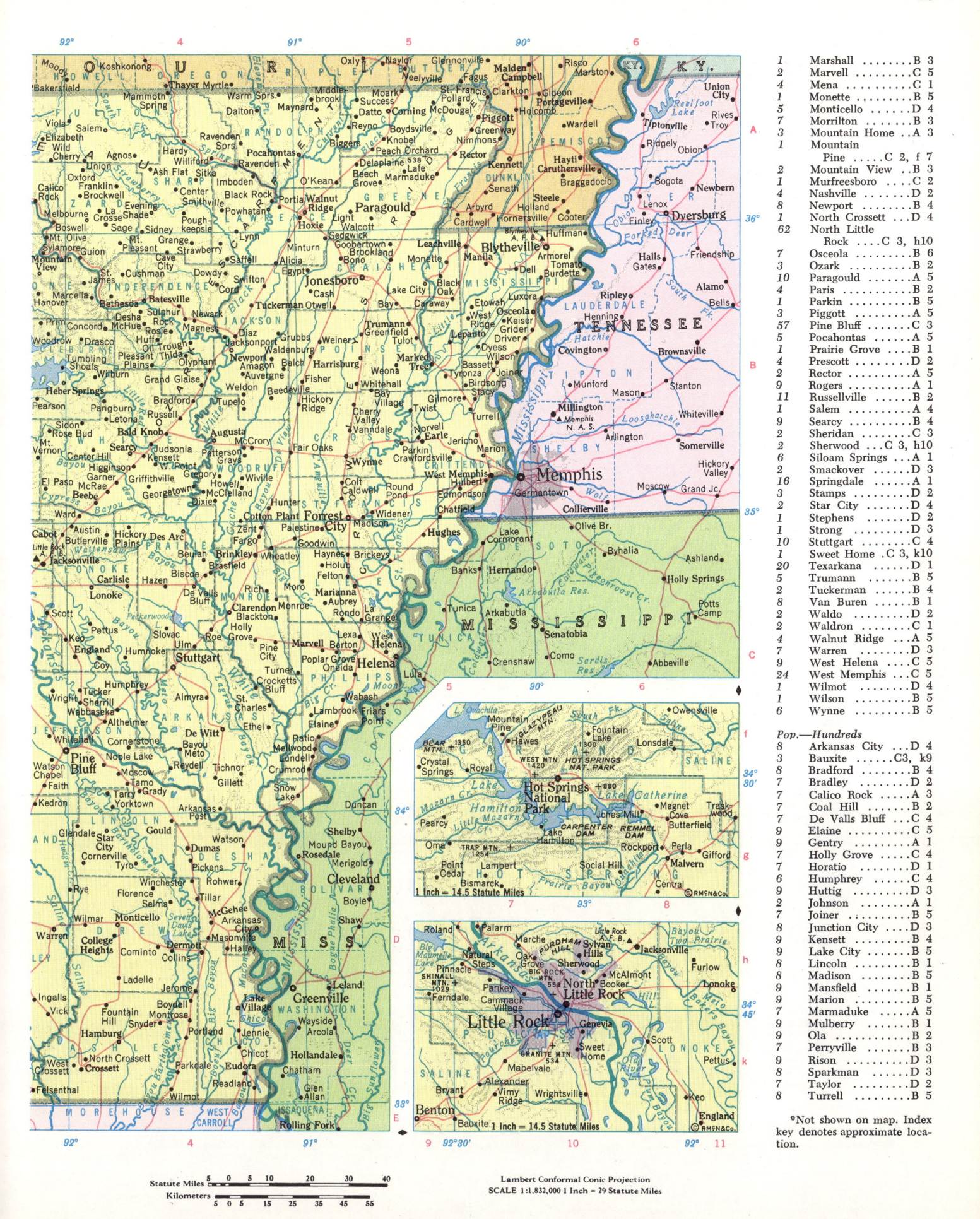

1	Marshall	B 3
2	Marvell	C 5
4	Mena	C 1
1	Monette	B 5
7	Monticello	D 4
3	Morrilton	B 3
1	Mountain Home	A 3
	Mountain	
	Pine	C 2, f 7
3	Mountain View	B 3
1	Murfreesboro	C 2
4	Nashville	D 2
8	Newport	B 4
1	North Crossett	D 4
62	North Little	
	Rock	C 3, h10
7	Osceola	B 6
3	Ozark	B 2
10	Paragould	A 5
4	Paris	B 2
1	Parkin	B 5
3	Piggott	A 5
57	Pine Bluff	C 3
5	Pocahontas	A 5
1	Prairie Grove	B 1
4	Prescott	D 2
5	Rector	A 5
9	Rogers	A 1
11	Russellville	B 2
1	Salem	A 4
9	Searcy	B 4
2	Sheridan	C 3
2	Sherwood	C 3, h10
6	Siloam Springs	A 1
2	Smackover	D 3
16	Springdale	A 1
3	Stamps	D 2
2	Star City	D 4
1	Stephens	D 2
1	Strong	D 3
10	Stuttgart	C 4
1	Sweet Home	C 3, k10
20	Texarkana	D 1
5	Trumann	B 5
2	Tuckerman	B 4
8	Van Buren	B 1
2	Waldo	D 2
2	Waldron	C 1
4	Walnut Ridge	A 5
7	Warren	D 3
7	West Helena	C 5
24	West Memphis	C 5
1	Wilmot	D 4
1	Wilson	B 5
6	Wynne	B 5

Pop.—Hundreds

8	Arkansas City	D 4
3	Bauxite	C3, k9
7	Bradford	B 4
7	Bradley	D 2
7	Calico Rock	A 3
7	Coal Hill	B 2
7	De Valls Bluff	C 4
9	Elaine	C 5
9	Gentry	A 1
7	Holly Grove	C 4
7	Horatio	D 1
6	Humphrey	C 4
9	Huttig	D 3
2	Johnson	A 1
7	Joiner	B 5
7	Junction City	D 3
9	Kensett	B 4
9	Lake City	B 5
9	Lincoln	B 1
8	Madison	B 5
9	Mansfield	B 1
9	Marion	B 5
7	Marmaduke	A 5
9	Mulberry	B 1
9	Ola	B 2
7	Perryville	B 3
9	Rison	D 3
8	Sparkman	D 3
7	Taylor	D 2
8	Turrell	B 5

°Not shown on map. Index key denotes approximate location.

Statute Miles
Kilometers

Lambert Conformal Conic Projection
SCALE 1:1,832,000 1 Inch = 29 Statute Miles

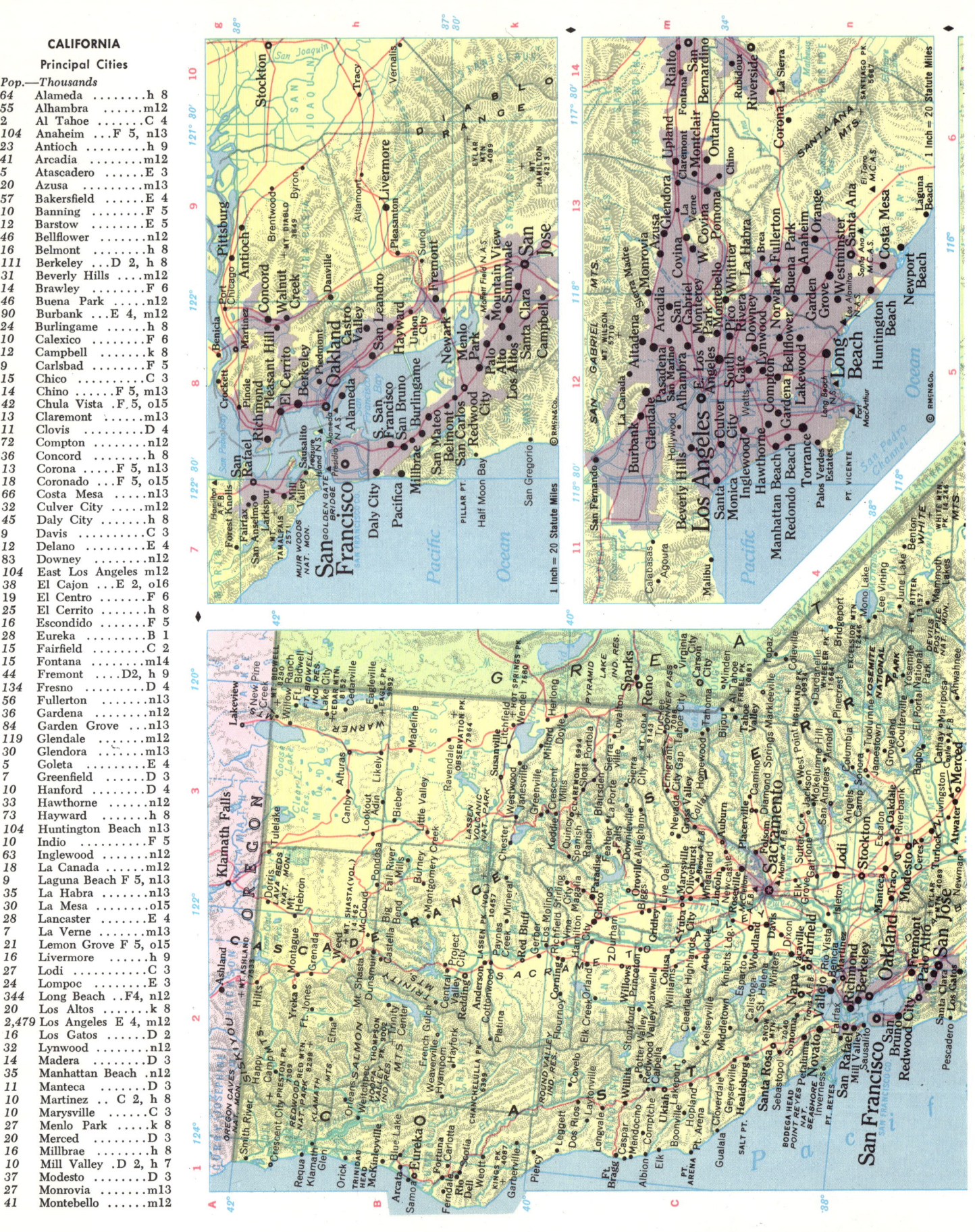

CALIFORNIA

CALIFORNIA
Principal Cities

Pop.—Thousands

Pop	City	Ref
64	Alameda	h 8
55	Alhambra	m12
2	Al Tahoe	C 4
104	Anaheim	F 5, n13
23	Antioch	h 9
41	Arcadia	m12
5	Atascadero	E 3
20	Azusa	m13
57	Bakersfield	E 4
10	Banning	F 5
12	Barstow	E 5
46	Bellflower	n12
16	Belmont	h 8
111	Berkeley	D 2, h 8
31	Beverly Hills	m12
14	Brawley	F 6
46	Buena Park	n12
90	Burbank	E 4, m12
24	Burlingame	h 8
10	Calexico	F 6
12	Campbell	k 8
9	Carlsbad	F 5
15	Chico	C 3
14	Chino	F 5, m13
42	Chula Vista	F 5, o15
13	Claremont	m13
11	Clovis	D 4
72	Compton	n12
36	Concord	h 8
13	Corona	F 5, n13
18	Coronado	F 5, o15
66	Costa Mesa	n13
32	Culver City	m12
45	Daly City	h 8
9	Davis	C 3
12	Delano	E 4
83	Downey	n12
104	East Los Angeles	m12
38	El Cajon	E 2, o16
19	El Centro	F 6
25	El Cerrito	h 8
16	Escondido	F 5
28	Eureka	B 1
15	Fairfield	C 2
15	Fontana	m14
44	Fremont	D2, h 9
134	Fresno	D 4
56	Fullerton	n13
36	Gardena	n12
84	Garden Grove	n13
119	Glendale	m12
30	Glendora	m13
5	Goleta	E 4
7	Greenfield	D 3
10	Hanford	D 4
33	Hawthorne	n12
73	Hayward	h 8
104	Huntington Beach	n13
10	Indio	F 5
63	Inglewood	n12
18	La Canada	m12
9	Laguna Beach	F 5, n13
35	La Habra	n13
30	La Mesa	o15
28	Lancaster	E 4
7	La Verne	m13
21	Lemon Grove	F 5, o15
16	Livermore	h 9
27	Lodi	C 3
24	Lompoc	E 3
344	Long Beach	F4, n12
20	Los Altos	k 8
2,479	Los Angeles	E 4, m12
16	Los Gatos	D 2
32	Lynwood	n12
14	Madera	D 3
35	Manhattan Beach	n12
11	Manteca	D 3
10	Martinez	C 2, h 8
10	Marysville	C 3
27	Menlo Park	k 8
20	Merced	D 3
16	Millbrae	h 8
10	Mill Valley	D 2, h 7
37	Modesto	D 3
27	Monrovia	m13
41	Montebello	m12

25	Monterey	D 3
38	Monterey Park	..m12
31	Mountain View	..k 8
22	Napa	C 2
33	National City	F 5, o15
3	Newman	D 3
10	Newark	h 8
27	Newport Beach	F 5, n13
18	Novato	C 2
368	Oakland	D 2, h 8
32	Oceanside	F 5
21	Oildale	E 4
47	Ontario	E 5, m13
67	Orange	n13
58	Oxnard	E 4
12	Pacific Grove	D 3
7	Palmdale	E 4
13	Palm Springs	F 5
52	Palo Alto	D 2, k 8
11	Paradise	C 3
116	Pasadena	E 4, m12
18	Petaluma	C 2
11	Piedmont	h 8
19	Pittsburg	g 9
22	Pleasant Hill	h 8
67	Pomona	E 5, m13
8	Porterville	D 4
11	Port Hueneme	E 4
13	Redding	B 2
27	Redlands	E 5
47	Redondo Beach	..n12
46	Redwood City	D 2, k 8
72	Richmond	D 2, h 8
84	Riverside	F 5, n14
13	Roseville	C 3
258	Sacramento	C 3
52	Salinas	D 3
12	San Anselmo	h 7
92	San Bernardino	E 5, m14
29	San Bruno	D 2, h 8
21	San Carlos	k 8
13	San Clemente	F 5
573	San Diego	F 5, o15
16	San Fernando	m12
740	San Francisco	D 2, h 8
23	San Gabriel	m12
204	San Jose	D 3, k 9
66	San Leandro	h 8
20	San Luis Obispo	.E 3
14	San Marino	m12
70	San Mateo	h 8
20	San Rafael	D 2, h 7
100	Santa Ana	F 5, n13
59	Santa Barbara	E 4
59	Santa Clara	D 2, k 9
26	Santa Cruz	D 2
20	Santa Maria	E 3
83	Santa Monica	m12
13	Santa Paula	E 4
42	Santa Rosa	C 2
10	Sierra Madre	m12
54	South Gate	n12
39	South San Francisco	h 8
13	Spring Valley	o16
98	Stockton	D 3, h10
53	Sunnyvale	k 8
101	Torrance	n12
14	Tracy	D 3, h10
14	Tulare	D 4
10	Ukiah	C 2
16	Upland	E 5, m13
11	Vacaville	C 3
61	Vallejo	C 2
29	Ventura	E 4
21	Visalia	D 4
20	Vista	F 5
23	Walnut Creek	h 8
13	Watsonville	D 3
60	West Covina	m13
98	Westminster	n12
34	Whittier	F 4, n12
14	Woodland	C 3
12	Yuba City	C 3

°Not shown on map. Index key denotes approximate location.

Lambert Conformal Conic Projection
SCALE 1:3,733,000 1 Inch = 59 Statute Miles

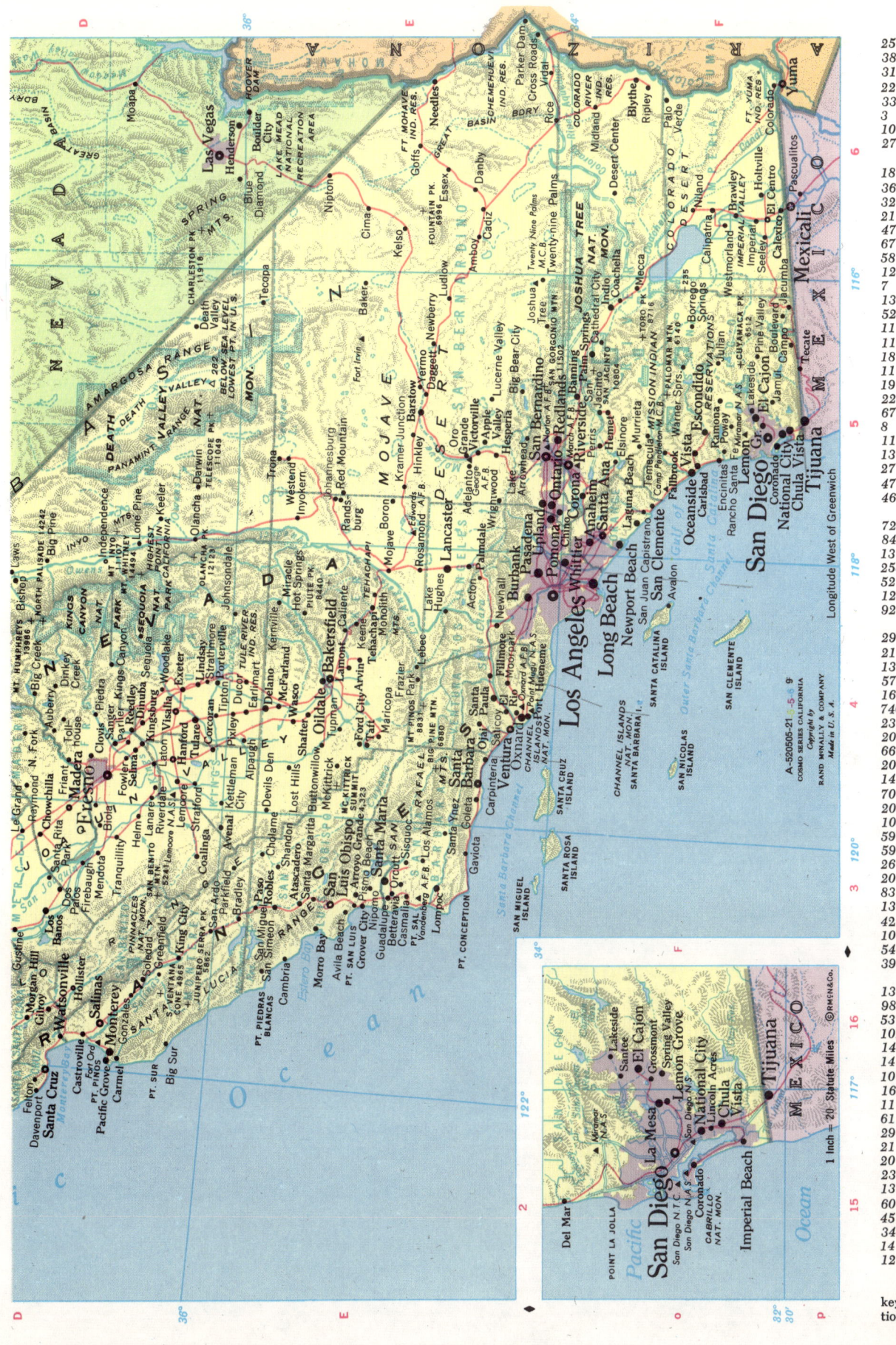

38 / TODAY'S WORLD

CALIFORNIA

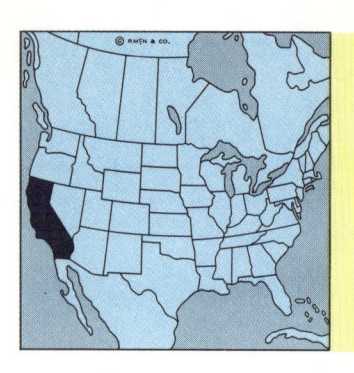

Capital: Sacramento

Area: 158,693 square miles (including 2,156 square miles of inland water)

Area rank: 3rd

Population (1970): 19,751,000

Population rank: 1st

Largest city: Los Angeles

Statehood: September 9, 1850; 31st state

Representatives: 38

Electoral votes: 40

California is nicknamed the Golden State, its state flower is the golden poppy, and the entrance to its finest harbor is called the Golden Gate. Gold-rush days are the best-known period of California history. Gold-pebbled stream beds, the glamour of Hollywood, a romantic past, snow-topped mountains, rushing streams, the sparkling blue Pacific, mysterious deserts, warm winters, and refreshingly cool summers—these make up California as most of the world dreams of it. This glamorous picture is true, but it omits some important facts.

California still has gold mines, but the unromantic oil and gas it produces in a year are worth more than 400 times as much as the gold. Its more spectacular crops—oranges, dates, olives, almonds, avocados—are outranked by prosaic tomatoes, lettuce, potatoes, apples, grapes, and hay.

Two rows of mountains run nearly the length of California. On the east are the high, snowy Sierras and Cascades. The Coast Ranges, in most places, rise almost directly from the ocean. Between the two mountain systems is the Central Valley, hot and dry, but fine farming land when it is irrigated. The Sacramento River from the north meets the San Joaquin from the south in the valley and they flow together into San Francisco Bay. The Bay and the low mountains give the city of San Francisco a setting of breath-taking beauty, besides providing it with one of the best harbors in the world.

The southern coast is the Mediterranean region of California, with less than 20 inches of rain in a year, falling mostly in winter. In 1789, the Spanish village that grew into the city of Los Angeles was founded there. Hollywood is part of it, but so is the choking smog, caused when a layer of cold air from above forces smoke and car exhaust to hover over the city.

East of Los Angeles, over the mountains, is the desert. At the southern end, irrigated from the Colorado River, is the Imperial Valley, a fabulous producer of winter vegetables. To the east is Death Valley, far below sea level and almost lifeless. Contrasted with the dry south is the moist, green, forest-covered north.

The stern grandeur of El Capitan's sheer granite cliffs and the delicate beauty of Bridal Veil Falls provide a dramatic landscape in Yosemite National Park.

The spectacular Golden Gate Bridge of San Francisco crosses the Golden Gate, the waterway linking San Francisco Bay with the Pacific Ocean.

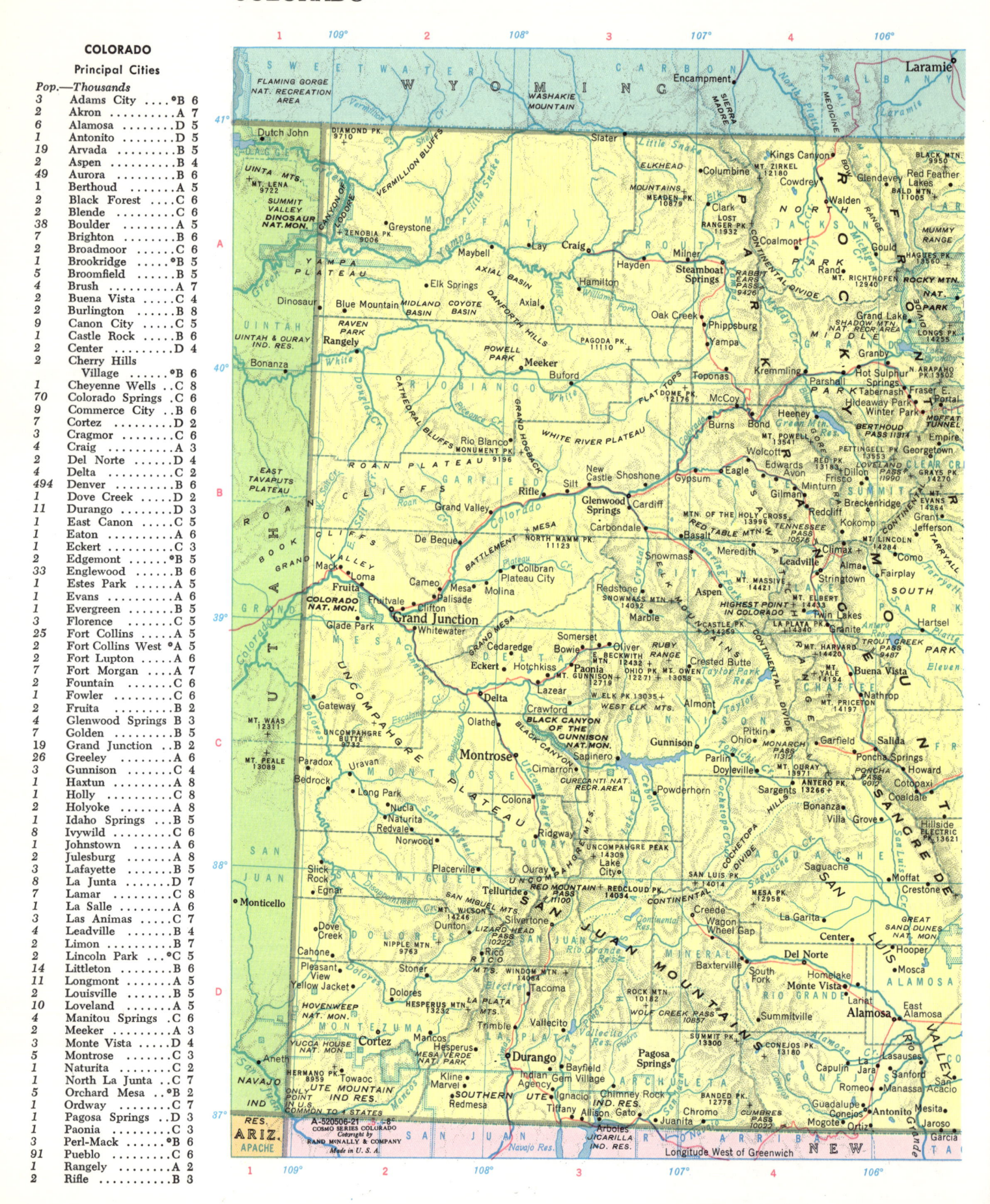

COLORADO

COLORADO
Principal Cities
Pop.—Thousands

Pop	City	Grid
3	Adams City	°B 6
2	Akron	A 7
6	Alamosa	D 5
1	Antonito	D 5
19	Arvada	B 5
2	Aspen	B 4
49	Aurora	B 6
1	Berthoud	A 5
2	Black Forest	C 6
2	Blende	C 6
38	Boulder	A 5
7	Brighton	B 6
2	Broadmoor	C 6
1	Brookridge	°B 5
5	Broomfield	B 5
4	Brush	A 7
2	Buena Vista	C 4
2	Burlington	B 8
9	Canon City	C 5
1	Castle Rock	B 6
2	Center	D 4
2	Cherry Hills Village	°B 6
1	Cheyenne Wells	C 8
70	Colorado Springs	C 6
9	Commerce City	B 6
7	Cortez	D 2
3	Cragmor	C 6
4	Craig	A 3
2	Del Norte	D 4
4	Delta	C 2
494	Denver	B 6
1	Dove Creek	D 2
11	Durango	D 3
1	East Canon	C 5
1	Eaton	A 6
1	Eckert	C 3
2	Edgemont	°B 5
33	Englewood	B 6
1	Estes Park	A 5
1	Evans	A 6
1	Evergreen	B 5
3	Florence	C 5
25	Fort Collins	A 5
2	Fort Collins West	°A 5
2	Fort Lupton	A 6
7	Fort Morgan	A 7
2	Fountain	C 6
1	Fowler	C 6
2	Fruita	B 2
4	Glenwood Springs	B 3
7	Golden	B 5
19	Grand Junction	B 2
26	Greeley	A 6
3	Gunnison	C 4
1	Haxtun	A 8
1	Holly	C 8
2	Holyoke	A 8
1	Idaho Springs	B 5
8	Ivywild	C 6
1	Johnstown	A 6
2	Julesburg	A 8
3	Lafayette	B 5
8	La Junta	D 7
7	Lamar	C 8
1	La Salle	A 6
3	Las Animas	C 7
4	Leadville	B 4
2	Limon	B 7
2	Lincoln Park	°C 5
14	Littleton	B 6
11	Longmont	A 5
2	Louisville	B 5
10	Loveland	A 5
4	Manitou Springs	C 6
2	Meeker	A 3
3	Monte Vista	D 4
5	Montrose	C 3
1	Naturita	C 2
1	North La Junta	C 7
5	Orchard Mesa	°B 2
1	Ordway	C 7
1	Pagosa Springs	D 3
1	Paonia	C 3
3	Perl-Mack	°B 6
91	Pueblo	C 6
1	Rangely	A 2
2	Rifle	B 3

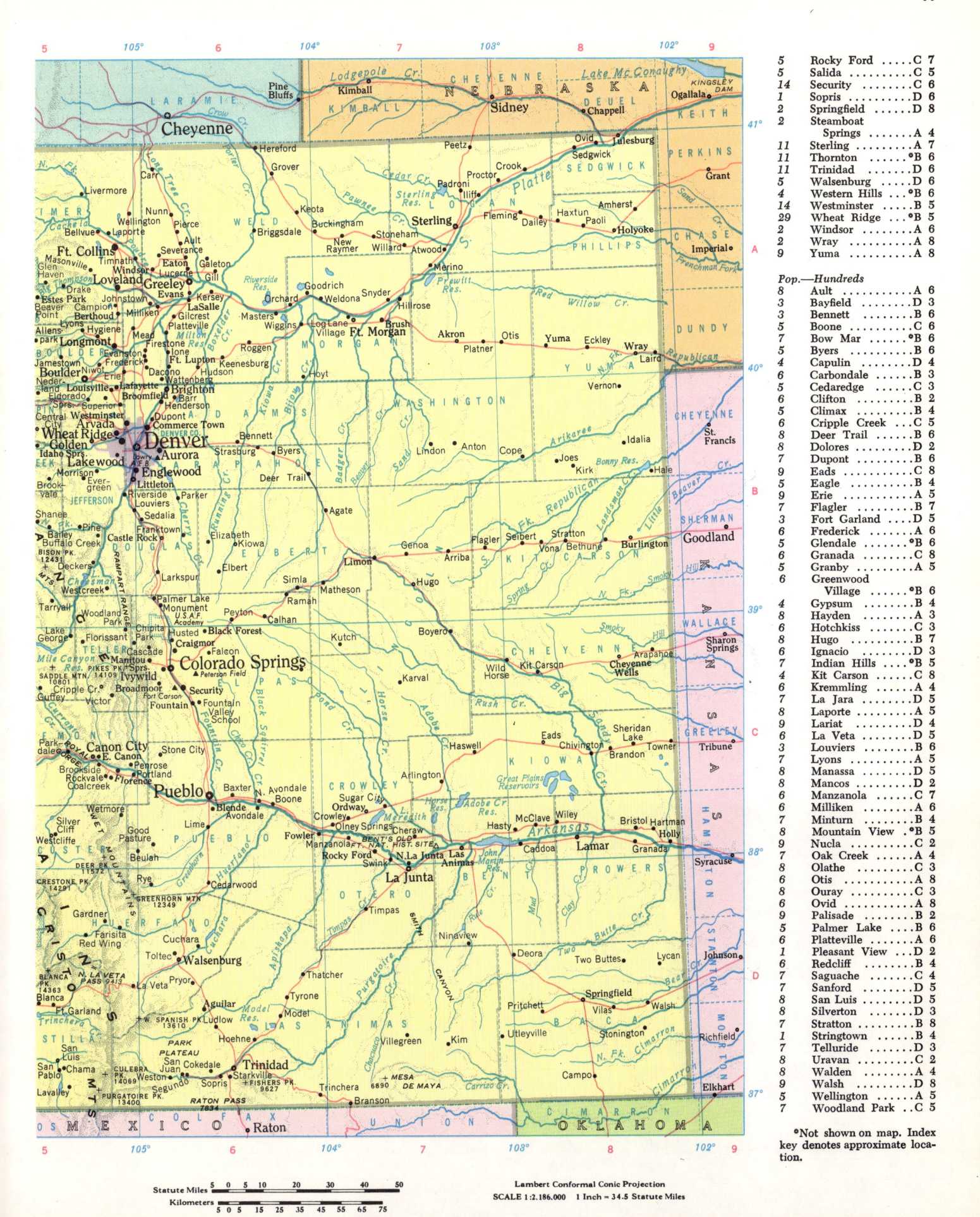

Pop. (Hundreds)	City	Index
5	Rocky Ford	C 7
5	Salida	C 5
14	Security	C 6
1	Sopris	D 6
2	Springfield	D 8
2	Steamboat Springs	A 4
11	Sterling	A 7
11	Thornton	*B 6
11	Trinidad	D 6
5	Walsenburg	D 6
4	Western Hills	*B 6
14	Westminster	B 5
29	Wheat Ridge	*B 5
2	Windsor	A 6
2	Wray	A 8
9	Yuma	A 8

Pop.—Hundreds

Pop.	City	Index
8	Ault	A 6
3	Bayfield	D 3
3	Bennett	B 6
7	Boone	C 6
7	Bow Mar	*B 6
5	Byers	B 6
6	Capulin	D 4
5	Carbondale	B 3
6	Cedaredge	C 3
5	Clifton	B 2
5	Climax	B 4
6	Cripple Creek	C 5
8	Deer Trail	B 6
8	Dolores	D 2
7	Dupont	B 6
9	Eads	C 8
5	Eagle	B 4
9	Erie	A 5
5	Flagler	B 7
3	Fort Garland	D 5
6	Frederick	A 6
5	Glendale	*B 5
6	Granada	C 8
5	Granby	A 5
6	Greenwood Village	*B 6
4	Gypsum	B 4
8	Hayden	A 3
5	Hotchkiss	C 3
8	Hugo	B 7
6	Ignacio	D 3
5	Indian Hills	*B 5
4	Kit Carson	C 8
6	Kremmling	A 4
5	La Jara	D 5
8	Laporte	A 5
9	Lariat	A 5
6	La Veta	D 5
7	Lyons	A 5
5	Manassa	D 5
8	Mancos	D 2
6	Manzanola	C 7
6	Milliken	A 6
7	Minturn	B 4
8	Mountain View	*B 5
9	Nucla	C 2
7	Oak Creek	A 4
8	Olathe	C 3
6	Otis	A 8
8	Ouray	C 3
6	Ovid	A 8
9	Palisade	B 2
5	Palmer Lake	B 6
6	Platteville	A 6
1	Pleasant View	D 2
7	Redcliff	B 4
7	Saguache	C 4
7	Sanford	D 5
8	San Luis	D 5
8	Silverton	D 3
7	Stratton	B 8
1	Stringtown	B 4
7	Telluride	D 3
8	Uravan	C 2
8	Walden	A 4
8	Walsh	D 8
7	Wellington	A 5
7	Woodland Park	C 5

*Not shown on map. Index key denotes approximate location.

COLORADO

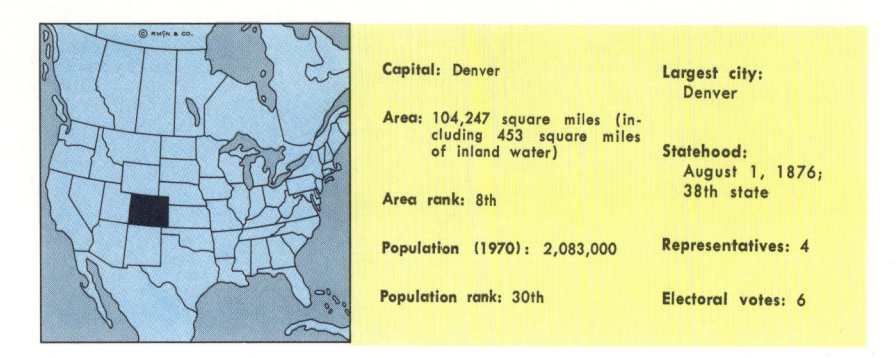

Capital: Denver

Area: 104,247 square miles (including 453 square miles of inland water)

Area rank: 8th

Population (1970): 2,083,000

Population rank: 30th

Largest city: Denver

Statehood: August 1, 1876; 38th state

Representatives: 4

Electoral votes: 6

Rugged mountain chains crowned with lofty summits dominate western Colorado. In this springtime scene, White House Mountain in the San Juan Range is topped with snow.

At the east, a little more than a third of Colorado is on the Great Plains. Through the center run the Rocky Mountains, range after range. At the west, occupying about a fifth of the state, is a region of rough plateaus.

From the eastern edge of the state, the plain slopes upward to the foothills of the mountains. Denver, the capital, is on the plains but it is called, with truth, the mile-high city. The mountains have many peaks that rise above 14,000 feet. Outflowing rivers prove that Colorado is higher than its neighbor states.

Where the surface is not barren rock, snow-covered mountains, or almost perpendicular slopes, most of Colorado is grazing land. The Great Plains are dry and covered with clumps of short bunchgrass. The mountains have high, grassy basins, called parks, and green mountain meadows that are covered with flowers. The western plateau region is very dry, but most of it is lightly forested, mainly with pine and juniper; it has enough grass for grazing.

On the plains, especially at the east and north, fields of wheat and sorghum break into the grazing land. Except in these areas, farming depends upon irrigation.

In 1858, gold was discovered in the eastern Rockies, and fortune seekers, prospectors, miners, and others who hoped to profit if the gold hunters profited, rushed into Colorado. The first settlement, called Auroria, part of the present site of Denver, became the center of Colorado mining activities. The state was admitted to the Union in 1876.

Most of the larger cities of Colorado are in a line at the edge of the Great Plains, north and south of Denver. Greeley, at the north, is a trade center for a large irrigated area; Colorado Springs is a transportation and tourist center; Pueblo, farther south, is the marketing point for an irrigated region.

Colorado is probably known best to the rest of the country as vacation country. It has ski resorts, dude ranches, beautiful camp sites, trout streams, abundant wildlife, fine mountain air, and magnificent scenery.

Colorado \ 43

Future Air Force officers parade before the Chapel Building at the U.S. Air Force Academy near Colorado Springs.

44 / TODAY'S WORLD

Hartford is an important link in today's bustling East Coast "megalopolis," a continuous area of settlement along railroads and expressways (rear) from New England to Virginia.

CONNECTICUT

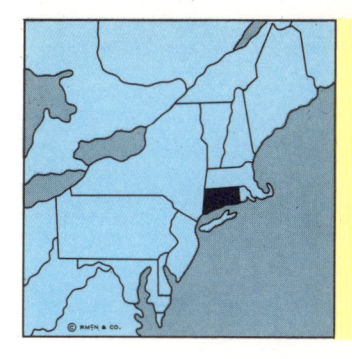

Capital: Hartford	**Largest city:** Hartford
Area: 5,009 square miles (including 139 square miles of inland water)	**Statehood:** January 9, 1788; 5th state
Area rank: 48th	**Representatives:** 6
Population (1970): 3,025,000	**Electoral votes:** 8
Population rank: 24th	

Connecticut has no coal, oil, nor gas. It has no minerals at all except rock and clay and a small deposit of beryllium. It has small salt-water fisheries, smaller than the value of neighboring Rhode Island's. It has waterfalls, which used to be suitable for running factories, and a small amount of flat, fertile land.

Yet Connecticut, the forty-eighth state in area, ranks twenty-fourth in population. Its inhabitants enjoy one of the highest per capita incomes in the country, almost 25 per cent above the national average.

Connecticut's recorded history goes back to 1614 when a Dutch trader explored the coast and the principal inland waterway, the Connecticut River. Colonists from Massachusetts Bay settled at Hartford and two nearby river sites in 1635. New Haven was established as a separate colony three years later, but the two groups soon joined. Connecticut was one of the thirteen original states.

Industrialization began back in colonial days. Yankee craftsmen in the towns of the Connecticut and Naugatuck valleys perfected formulas for brasses and bronzes; they made clocks, cutlery, and silverware. As farmers wearied of trying to till the thin soils of rocky Connecticut hillsides, they moved into the towns and went to work there. New Haven, Bridgeport, and New Britain began to produce machinery, hardware, and tools. In the nineteenth century, Colt made firearms in Hartford; Whitney, Goodyear, and Morse made important industrial inventions in New Haven.

Connecticut's location, between Boston and New York, made it easy to market the products its industries were turning out. The tradition of precision work earned it a reputation for quality and drew skilled manpower capable of adapting to a changing technology. Today, the state is one of the nation's leaders in manufacturing. Over forty per cent of the labor force is employed in the state's many large and small plants, in which a bewildering variety of things are made from steel, brass, aluminum, rubber, and plastic.

The state's agriculture is limited by its scarcity of good land, but a very special tobacco, used as wrapper leaves for cigars, is grown in the Connecticut River Valley. Dairy farms supply milk and butter for the populous cities.

Mystic Seaport, Connecticut, a re-created New England whaling village complete with ships, homes and shops.

CONNECTICUT

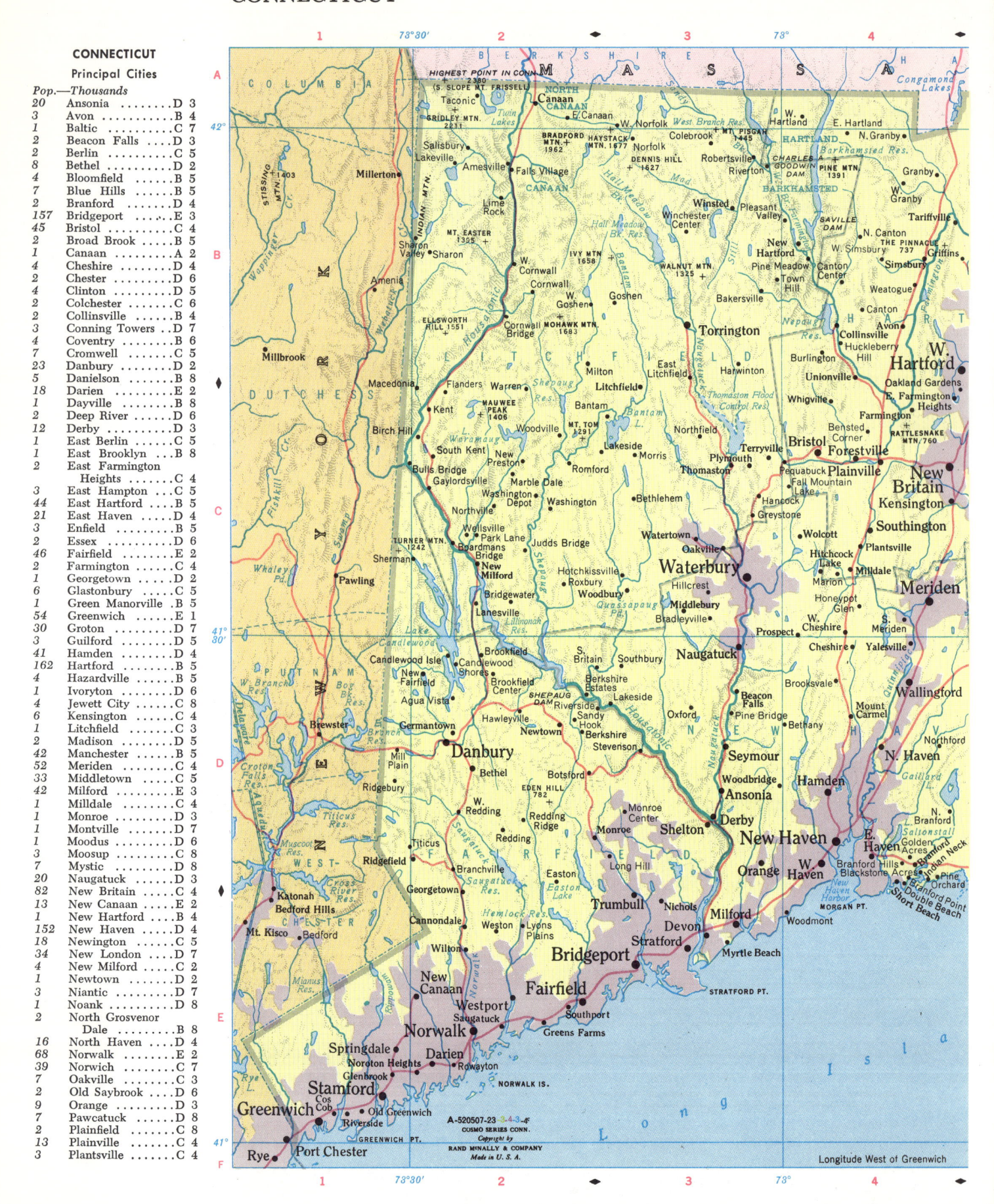

CONNECTICUT
Principal Cities

Pop.—Thousands		
20	Ansonia	D 3
3	Avon	B 4
1	Baltic	C 7
2	Beacon Falls	D 3
2	Berlin	C 5
8	Bethel	D 2
4	Bloomfield	B 5
7	Blue Hills	B 5
2	Branford	D 4
157	Bridgeport	E 3
45	Bristol	C 4
2	Broad Brook	B 5
1	Canaan	A 2
4	Cheshire	D 4
2	Chester	D 6
4	Clinton	D 5
2	Colchester	C 6
2	Collinsville	B 4
3	Conning Towers	D 7
4	Coventry	B 6
7	Cromwell	C 5
23	Danbury	D 2
5	Danielson	B 8
18	Darien	E 2
1	Dayville	B 8
2	Deep River	D 6
12	Derby	D 3
1	East Berlin	C 5
1	East Brooklyn	B 8
2	East Farmington Heights	C 4
3	East Hampton	C 5
44	East Hartford	B 5
21	East Haven	D 4
3	Enfield	B 5
2	Essex	D 6
46	Fairfield	E 2
2	Farmington	C 4
1	Georgetown	D 2
6	Glastonbury	C 5
1	Green Manorville	B 5
54	Greenwich	E 1
30	Groton	D 7
3	Guilford	D 5
41	Hamden	D 4
162	Hartford	B 5
4	Hazardville	B 5
1	Ivoryton	D 6
4	Jewett City	C 8
6	Kensington	C 4
1	Litchfield	C 3
2	Madison	D 5
42	Manchester	B 5
52	Meriden	C 4
33	Middletown	C 5
42	Milford	E 3
1	Milldale	C 4
1	Monroe	D 3
1	Montville	D 7
1	Moodus	D 6
3	Moosup	C 8
7	Mystic	D 8
20	Naugatuck	D 3
82	New Britain	C 4
13	New Canaan	E 2
1	New Hartford	B 4
152	New Haven	D 4
18	Newington	C 5
34	New London	D 7
4	New Milford	C 2
1	Newtown	D 2
3	Niantic	D 7
1	Noank	D 8
2	North Grosvenor Dale	B 8
16	North Haven	D 4
68	Norwalk	E 2
39	Norwich	C 7
7	Oakville	C 3
2	Old Saybrook	D 6
9	Orange	D 3
7	Pawcatuck	D 8
2	Plainfield	C 8
13	Plainville	C 4
3	Plantsville	C 4

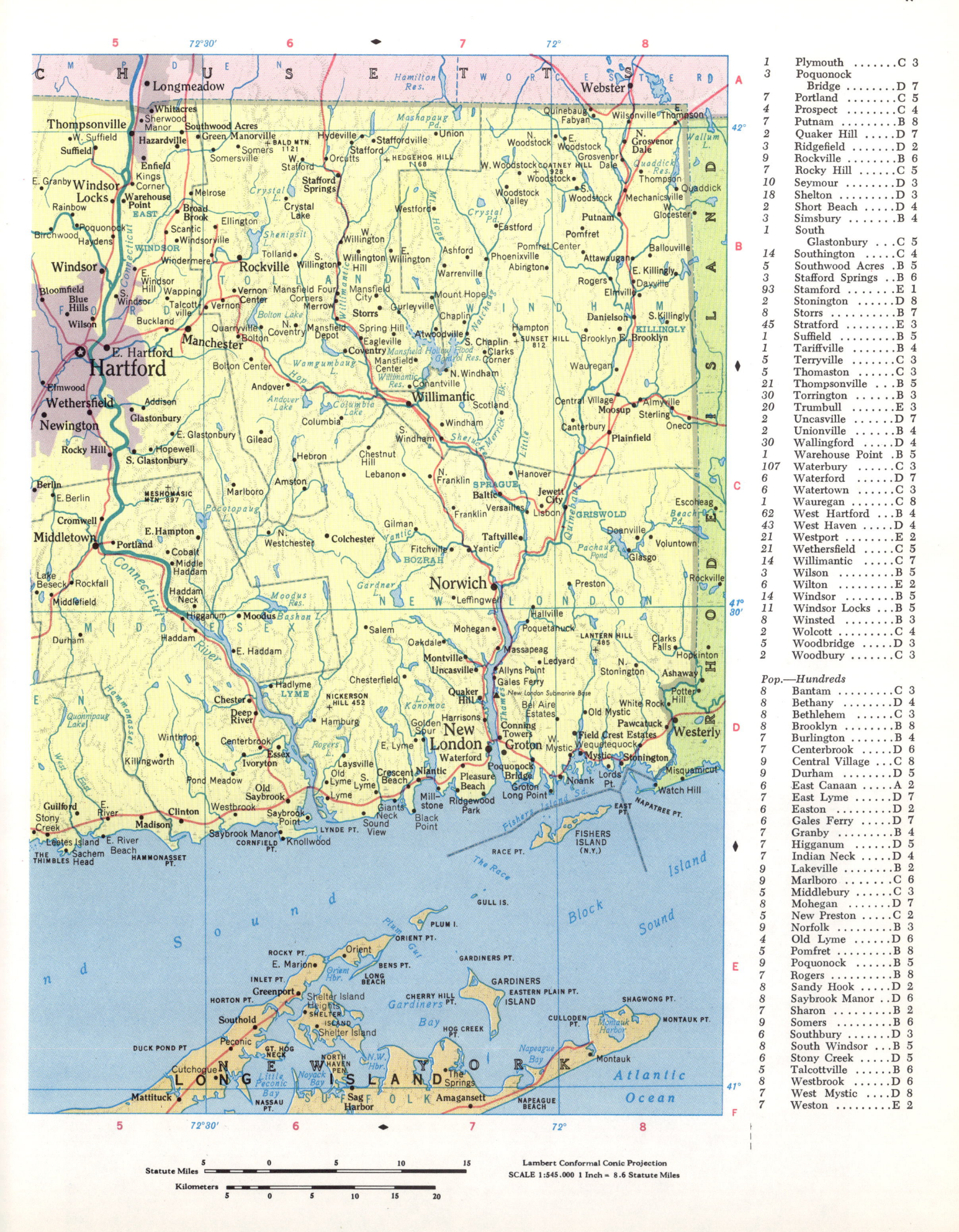

Pop.	Place	Grid
1	Plymouth	C 3
3	Poquonock Bridge	D 7
7	Portland	C 5
4	Prospect	C 4
7	Putnam	B 8
2	Quaker Hill	D 7
7	Ridgefield	D 2
9	Rockville	B 6
7	Rocky Hill	C 5
10	Seymour	D 3
18	Shelton	D 3
2	Short Beach	D 4
3	Simsbury	B 4
1	South Glastonbury	C 5
14	Southington	C 4
5	Southwood Acres	B 5
3	Stafford Springs	B 6
93	Stamford	E 1
2	Stonington	D 8
8	Storrs	C 7
45	Stratford	E 3
1	Suffield	B 5
1	Tariffville	B 4
5	Terryville	C 3
5	Thomaston	C 3
21	Thompsonville	B 5
30	Torrington	B 3
20	Trumbull	E 3
2	Uncasville	D 7
2	Unionville	B 4
30	Wallingford	D 4
1	Warehouse Point	B 5
107	Waterbury	C 3
6	Waterford	D 7
6	Watertown	C 3
1	Wauregan	C 8
62	West Hartford	B 4
43	West Haven	D 4
21	Westport	E 2
21	Wethersfield	C 5
14	Willimantic	C 7
3	Wilson	B 5
6	Wilton	E 2
14	Windsor	B 5
11	Windsor Locks	B 5
8	Winsted	B 3
4	Wolcott	C 4
5	Woodbridge	D 3
2	Woodbury	C 3

Pop.—Hundreds

Pop.	Place	Grid
8	Bantam	C 3
8	Bethany	D 4
8	Bethlehem	C 3
8	Brooklyn	B 8
7	Burlington	B 4
7	Centerbrook	D 6
9	Central Village	C 8
9	Durham	D 5
6	East Canaan	A 2
7	East Lyme	D 7
6	Easton	D 2
7	Gales Ferry	D 7
7	Granby	B 4
7	Higganum	D 5
7	Indian Neck	D 4
9	Lakeville	B 2
9	Marlboro	C 6
5	Middlebury	C 3
8	Mohegan	D 7
9	New Preston	C 2
9	Norfolk	B 3
4	Old Lyme	D 6
5	Pomfret	B 7
9	Poquonock	B 5
6	Rogers	B 8
8	Sandy Hook	D 2
8	Saybrook Manor	D 6
7	Sharon	B 2
9	Somers	B 6
6	Southbury	D 3
8	South Windsor	B 5
6	Stony Creek	D 5
6	Talcottville	B 6
8	Westbrook	D 6
7	West Mystic	D 8
7	Weston	E 2

DELAWARE

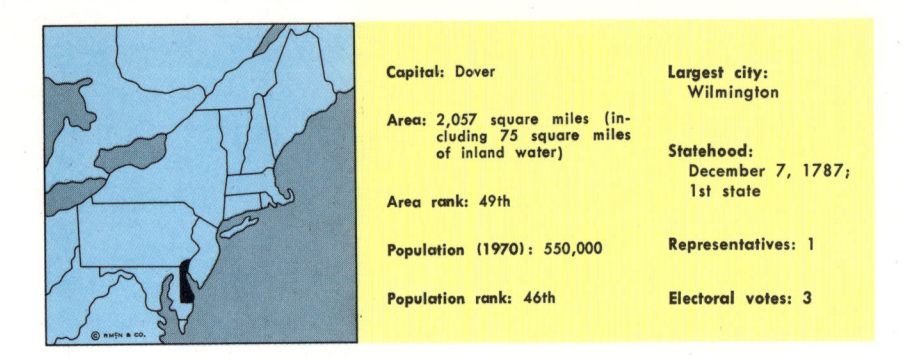

Capital: Dover

Area: 2,057 square miles (including 75 square miles of inland water)

Area rank: 49th

Population (1970): 550,000

Population rank: 46th

Largest city: Wilmington

Statehood: December 7, 1787; 1st state

Representatives: 1

Electoral votes: 3

In 1638, a group of Swedish settlers founded a settlement beside the Delaware River and called it Fort Christina. A Dutch expedition from New Amsterdam captured it in 1655. In 1664, the English took it over, along with New Netherland (New York). The area that is now Delaware was granted to William Penn in 1682 and became part of Pennsylvania; it was not made a separate colony until 1704. Delaware was one of the original thirteen states, and it was the first to ratify the constitution.

Dover became the capital in 1777, but Wilmington continued to be the largest and fastest-growing city in the state. It has become part of the industrial area that extends up the river beyond Philadelphia.

In 1802, E. I. du Pont decided to build a gunpowder mill at Wilmington. This was the beginning of the great du Pont chemical industry. The headquarters for the giant enterprise and some of the research laboratories are still there. Wilmington has become a city of diversified industries: shipbuilding, oil refining, and the manufacture of rubber and leather goods, iron and steel products, and textiles, among others.

Just outside of Wilmington is New Castle, a town of old houses and churches and cobbled streets. A main attraction for sightseers is the Old Dutch House, built in the seventeenth century.

Delaware is blessed with pleasant climate and a location favorable for farming, commerce, or manufacturing. Rain is well distributed through the year, 40 to 50 inches in all, and there is a long growing season.

Almost the entire state is coastal plain, flat and nearly featureless, and most of it is on the peninsula between Delaware Bay and Chesapeake Bay, which it shares with Maryland and Virginia. From the names of the three states, this piece of land is called the Delmarva Peninsula. In the entire area, farmers concentrate on producing food for the many cities of their region. There are dairy farms, especially in the north, and many poultry farmers raise broilers for the city markets. Vegetables, fruit, and feed crops grow everywhere in the state. Over 60 per cent of the people of Delaware live in the metropolitan area of Wilmington and in Dover, but more than half of the land in the state is in farms.

The Delaware Memorial Bridge, south of the city of Wilmington, arches across the wide waters of the Delaware River.

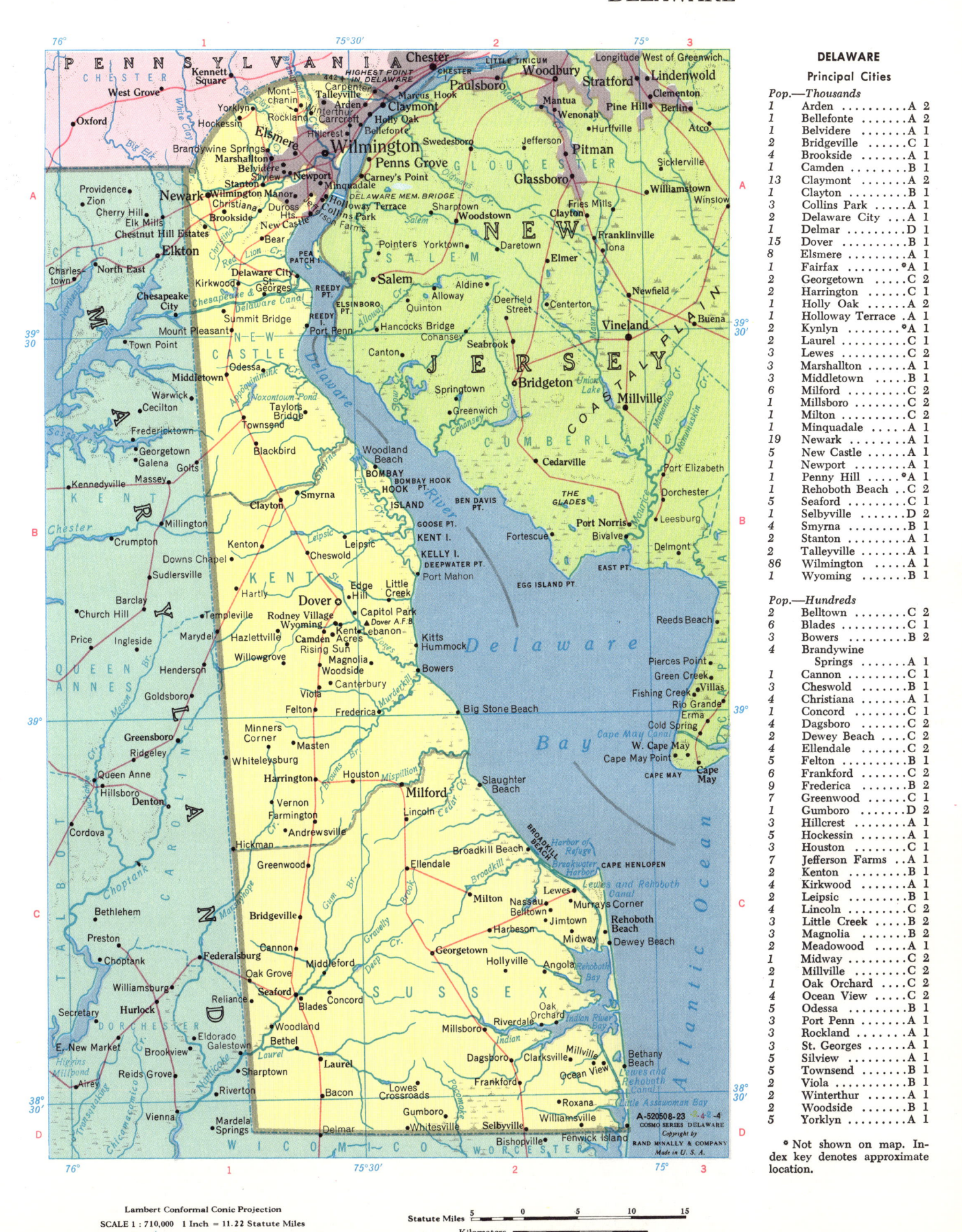

DELAWARE

DELAWARE
Principal Cities

Pop.—Thousands

Pop	City	Ref
1	Arden	A 2
1	Bellefonte	A 2
1	Belvidere	A 1
2	Bridgeville	C 1
4	Brookside	A 1
1	Camden	B 1
13	Claymont	A 2
1	Clayton	B 1
3	Collins Park	A 1
2	Delaware City	A 1
1	Delmar	D 1
15	Dover	B 1
8	Elsmere	A 1
1	Fairfax	*A 1
2	Georgetown	C 2
2	Harrington	C 1
1	Holly Oak	A 2
1	Holloway Terrace	A 1
2	Kynlyn	*A 1
2	Laurel	C 1
3	Lewes	C 2
3	Marshallton	A 1
3	Middletown	B 1
6	Milford	C 2
1	Millsboro	C 2
1	Milton	C 2
1	Minquadale	A 1
19	Newark	A 1
5	New Castle	A 1
1	Newport	A 1
1	Penny Hill	*A 1
1	Rehoboth Beach	C 2
5	Seaford	C 1
1	Selbyville	D 2
4	Smyrna	B 1
2	Stanton	A 1
2	Talleyville	A 1
86	Wilmington	A 1
1	Wyoming	B 1

Pop.—Hundreds

Pop	City	Ref
2	Belltown	C 2
6	Blades	C 1
3	Bowers	B 2
4	Brandywine Springs	A 1
1	Cannon	C 1
3	Cheswold	B 1
4	Christiana	A 1
1	Concord	C 1
4	Dagsboro	C 2
2	Dewey Beach	C 2
4	Ellendale	C 2
5	Felton	B 1
6	Frankford	C 2
9	Frederica	B 2
7	Greenwood	C 1
1	Gumboro	D 2
3	Hillcrest	A 1
5	Hockessin	A 1
3	Houston	C 1
7	Jefferson Farms	A 1
2	Kenton	B 1
4	Kirkwood	A 1
2	Leipsic	B 1
4	Lincoln	C 2
3	Little Creek	B 2
3	Magnolia	B 2
2	Meadowood	A 1
1	Midway	C 2
2	Millville	C 2
1	Oak Orchard	C 2
4	Ocean View	C 2
5	Odessa	B 1
3	Port Penn	A 1
3	Rockland	A 1
3	St. Georges	A 1
5	Silview	A 1
5	Townsend	B 1
2	Viola	B 1
2	Winterthur	A 1
2	Woodside	B 1
5	Yorklyn	A 1

* Not shown on map. Index key denotes approximate location.

Lambert Conformal Conic Projection
SCALE 1 : 710,000   1 Inch = 11.22 Statute Miles

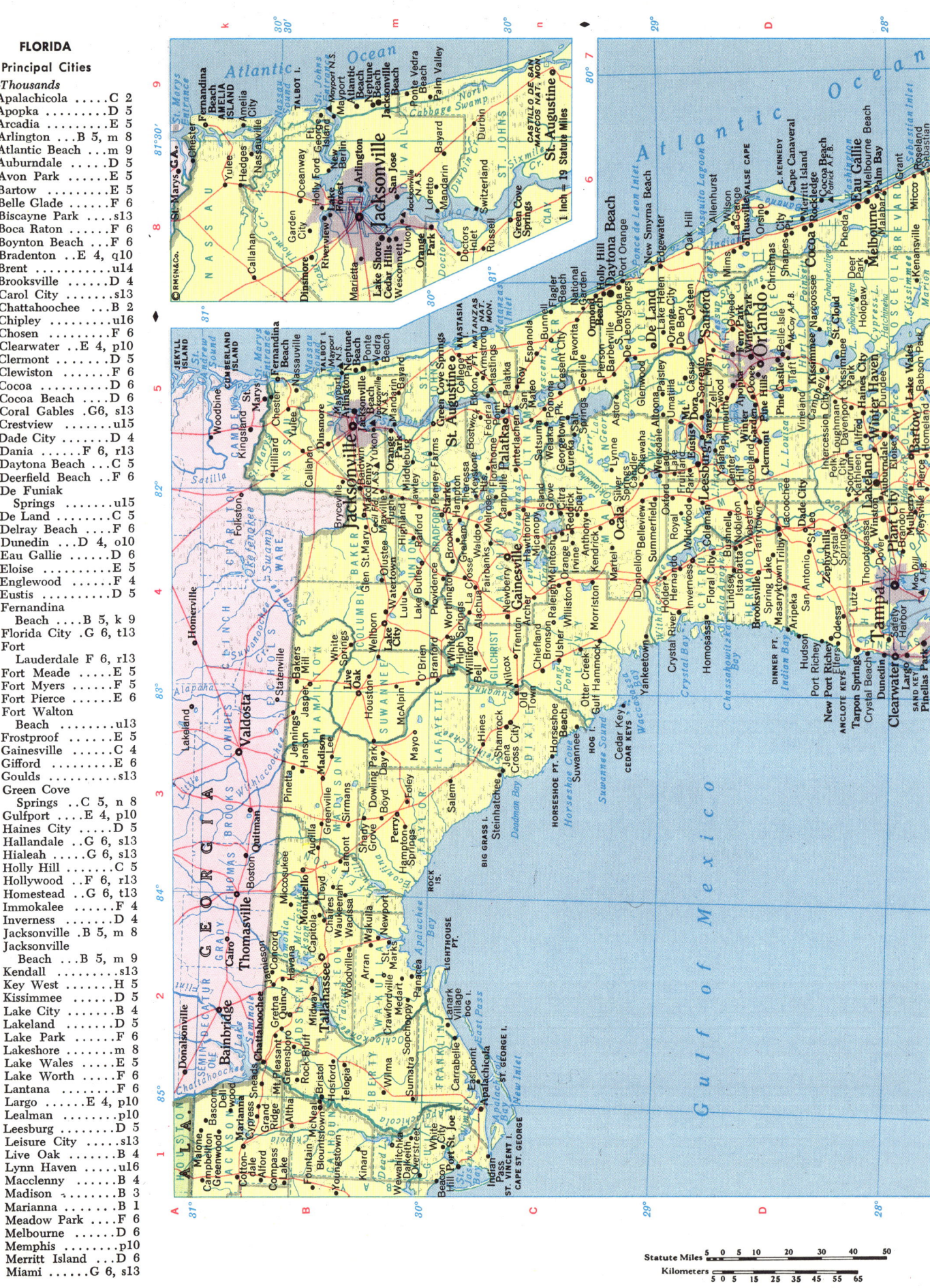

FLORIDA

FLORIDA
Principal Cities

Pop.—Thousands

Pop.	City	Grid
3	Apalachicola	C 2
4	Apopka	D 5
6	Arcadia	E 5
24	Arlington	B 5, m 8
3	Atlantic Beach	m 9
6	Auburndale	D 5
6	Avon Park	E 5
13	Bartow	E 5
11	Belle Glade	F 6
3	Biscayne Park	s13
7	Boca Raton	F 6
10	Boynton Beach	F 6
19	Bradenton	E 4, q10
7	Brent	u14
3	Brooksville	D 4
29	Carol City	s13
10	Chattahoochee	B 2
3	Chipley	u16
2	Chosen	F 6
35	Clearwater	E 4, p10
3	Clermont	D 5
3	Clewiston	F 6
12	Cocoa	D 6
3	Cocoa Beach	D 6
35	Coral Gables	G 6, s13
7	Crestview	u15
5	Dade City	D 4
7	Dania	F 6, r13
37	Daytona Beach	C 5
10	Deerfield Beach	F 6
5	De Funiak Springs	u15
11	De Land	C 5
12	Delray Beach	F 6
8	Dunedin	D 4, o10
12	Eau Gallie	D 6
3	Eloise	
4	Englewood	F 4
6	Eustis	D 5
7	Fernandina Beach	B 5, k 9
4	Florida City	G 6, t13
84	Fort Lauderdale	F 6, r13
4	Fort Meade	E 5
23	Fort Myers	F 5
25	Fort Pierce	E 6
12	Fort Walton Beach	u13
3	Frostproof	E 5
30	Gainesville	C 4
4	Gifford	E 6
5	Goulds	s13
4	Green Cove Springs	C 5, n 8
10	Gulfport	E 4, p10
9	Haines City	D 5
10	Hallandale	G 6, s13
67	Hialeah	G 6, s13
4	Holly Hill	C 5
35	Hollywood	F 6, r13
9	Homestead	G 6, t13
3	Immokalee	F 4
2	Inverness	D 4
201	Jacksonville	B 5, m 8
12	Jacksonville Beach	B 5, m 9
8	Kendall	s13
34	Key West	H 5
7	Kissimmee	D 5
9	Lake City	B 4
41	Lakeland	D 5
4	Lake Park	D 5
13	Lakeshore	m 8
8	Lake Wales	E 5
21	Lake Worth	F 6
5	Lantana	F 6
5	Largo	E 4, p10
20	Lealman	p10
11	Leesburg	D 5
3	Leisure City	s13
7	Live Oak	B 4
3	Lynn Haven	u16
3	Macclenny	B 4
3	Madison	B 3
7	Marianna	B 1
4	Meadow Park	
12	Melbourne	D 6
3	Memphis	p10
10	Merritt Island	D 6
292	Miami	G 6, s13

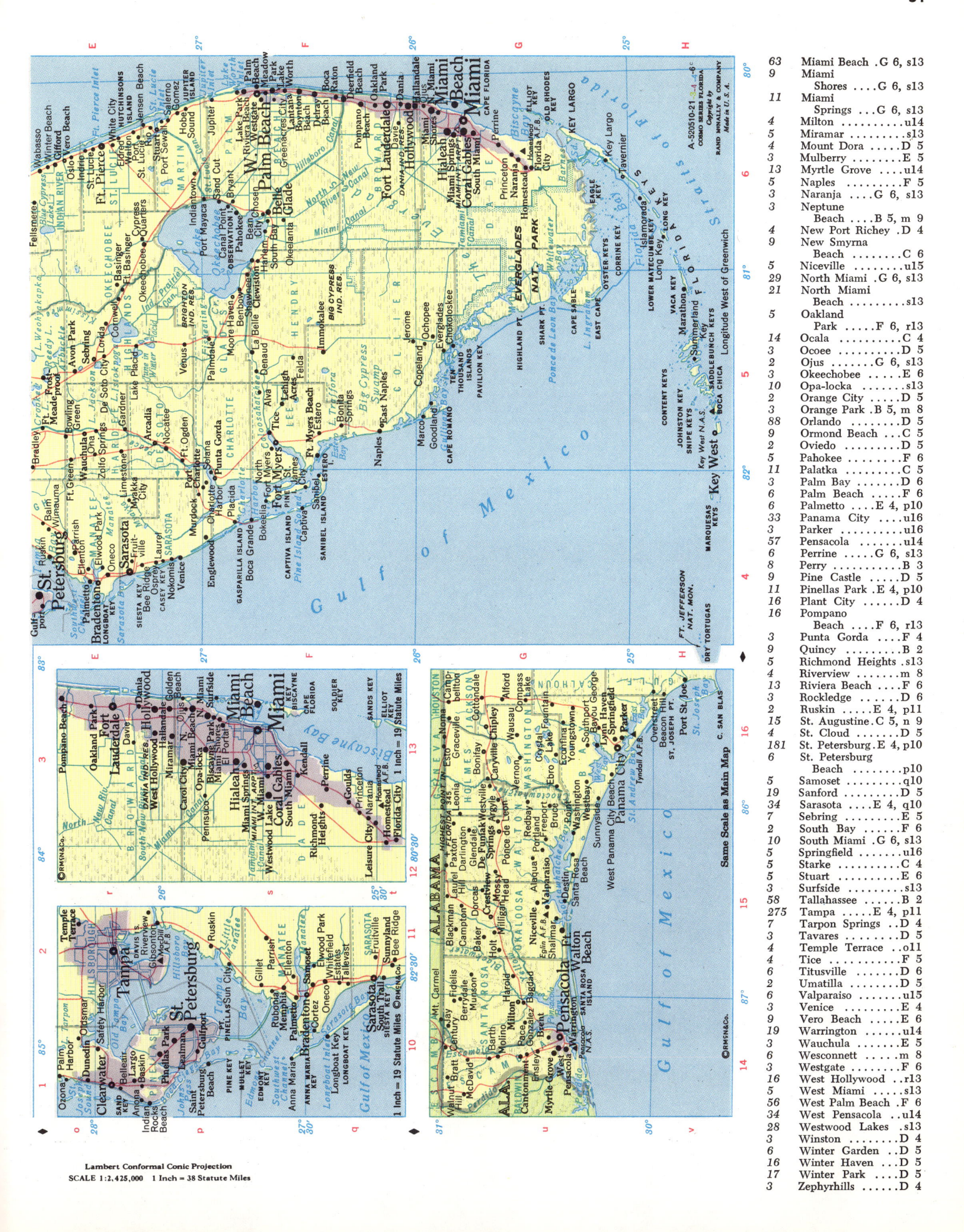

Pop.	Place	Ref.
63	Miami Beach	G 6, s13
9	Miami Shores	G 6, s13
11	Miami Springs	G 6, s13
4	Milton	u14
5	Miramar	s13
4	Mount Dora	D 5
3	Mulberry	E 5
13	Myrtle Grove	u14
5	Naples	F 5
3	Naranja	G 6, s13
3	Neptune Beach	B 5, m 9
4	New Port Richey	D 4
9	New Smyrna Beach	C 6
5	Niceville	u15
29	North Miami	G 6, s13
21	North Miami Beach	s13
5	Oakland Park	F 6, r13
14	Ocala	C 4
3	Ocoee	D 5
2	Ojus	G 6, s13
5	Okeechobee	E 6
10	Opa-locka	s13
2	Orange City	D 5
3	Orange Park	B 5, m 8
88	Orlando	D 5
9	Ormond Beach	C 5
2	Oviedo	D 5
5	Pahokee	F 6
11	Palatka	C 5
3	Palm Bay	D 6
6	Palm Beach	F 6
6	Palmetto	E 4, p10
33	Panama City	u16
3	Parker	u16
57	Pensacola	u14
6	Perrine	G 6, s13
8	Perry	B 3
9	Pine Castle	D 5
11	Pinellas Park	E 4, p10
16	Plant City	D 4
16	Pompano Beach	F 6, r13
3	Punta Gorda	F 4
9	Quincy	B 2
5	Richmond Heights	s13
4	Riverview	m 8
13	Riviera Beach	F 6
3	Rockledge	D 6
2	Ruskin	E 4, p11
15	St. Augustine	C 5, n 9
4	St. Cloud	D 5
181	St. Petersburg	E 4, p10
6	St. Petersburg Beach	p10
5	Samoset	q10
19	Sanford	D 5
34	Sarasota	E 4, q10
7	Sebring	E 5
2	South Bay	F 6
10	South Miami	G 6, s13
5	Springfield	u16
5	Starke	C 4
5	Stuart	E 6
3	Surfside	s13
58	Tallahassee	B 2
275	Tampa	E 4, p11
7	Tarpon Springs	D 4
3	Tavares	D 5
4	Temple Terrace	o11
4	Tice	F 5
6	Titusville	D 6
2	Umatilla	D 5
6	Valparaiso	u15
3	Venice	E 4
9	Vero Beach	E 6
19	Warrington	u14
3	Wauchula	D 5
6	Wesconnett	m 8
3	Westgate	F 6
16	West Hollywood	r13
5	West Miami	s13
56	West Palm Beach	F 6
34	West Pensacola	u14
28	Westwood Lakes	s13
3	Winston	D 4
6	Winter Garden	D 5
16	Winter Haven	D 5
17	Winter Park	D 5
3	Zephyrhills	D 4

Lambert Conformal Conic Projection
SCALE 1:2,425,000   1 Inch = 38 Statute Miles

FLORIDA

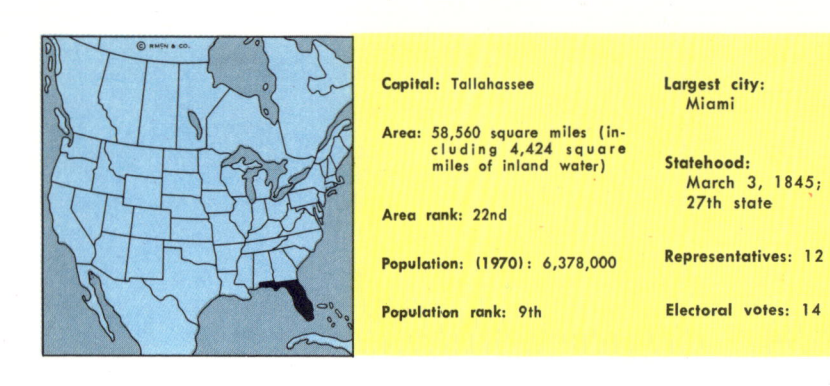

Capital: Tallahassee

Area: 58,560 square miles (including 4,424 square miles of inland water)

Area rank: 22nd

Population: (1970): 6,378,000

Population rank: 9th

Largest city: Miami

Statehood: March 3, 1845; 27th state

Representatives: 12

Electoral votes: 14

The Spanish explorer, Ponce de Leon, discovered Florida in 1513 while on a search for a "Fountain of Youth." Most Floridians today believe that their state, with its balmy sea breezes, white beachers, and sub-tropical climate is the nearest thing to a "Fountain of Youth."

St. Augustine, founded by Spanish settlers in 1565, is the oldest city in the United States. In spite of its early start, Florida did not prosper under Spain, and the population remained very small. It was still small in 1821 when Spain ceded Florida to the United States. In 1910, the population was only about three-quarters of a million. Now there are more than eight times as many people, but large areas have a sparse population.

Florida's location gives it warm winters, and the surrounding water usually keeps it from becoming excessively hot in summer. Its growing season is almost year-round, though winter cold fronts sometimes swing southward and bring severe frosts.

The state's famous citrus fruit comes mainly from an inland region that extends northeast from Tampa. From Lake Okeechobee south, most farmers specialize in growing winter vegetables. Just south of the lake is an area that specializes in sugar cane.

Large parts of Florida are open pine forest, dotted with swamps where palmetto palms and bald cypress trees crowd close together. The grassy areas are grazing land for cattle.

Industries are closely related to the state's resources. Sugar refining and the packing, canning, and freezing of fruits and vegetables depend on the farms. Forests support sawmills and large pulp and paper mills. The only valuable mineral product is phosphate, used in fertilizers.

To the whole world, Florida is famous as a resort area. Its many miles of fine beaches can be used the year round, except perhaps for an occasional day or two of cool weather. Every winter thousands of northern tourists come to vacation there.

Florida has many special attractions: deep-sea fishing and picturesque commercial fishing fleets; Seminole Indians in colorful costumes; the mysterious region of marshes and swamps called the Everglades; interesting wild animals and birds; the great naval base at Pensacola; and the launching site for missiles and satellites at Cape Kennedy.

Sponges, hanging in bunches to dry in the bright Florida sunlight, add a picturesque touch to many of the coastal harbor docks.

Modern resort hotels, their lavish splendor glittering in the sunlight, line the Atlantic seashore at Miami Beach.

GEORGIA

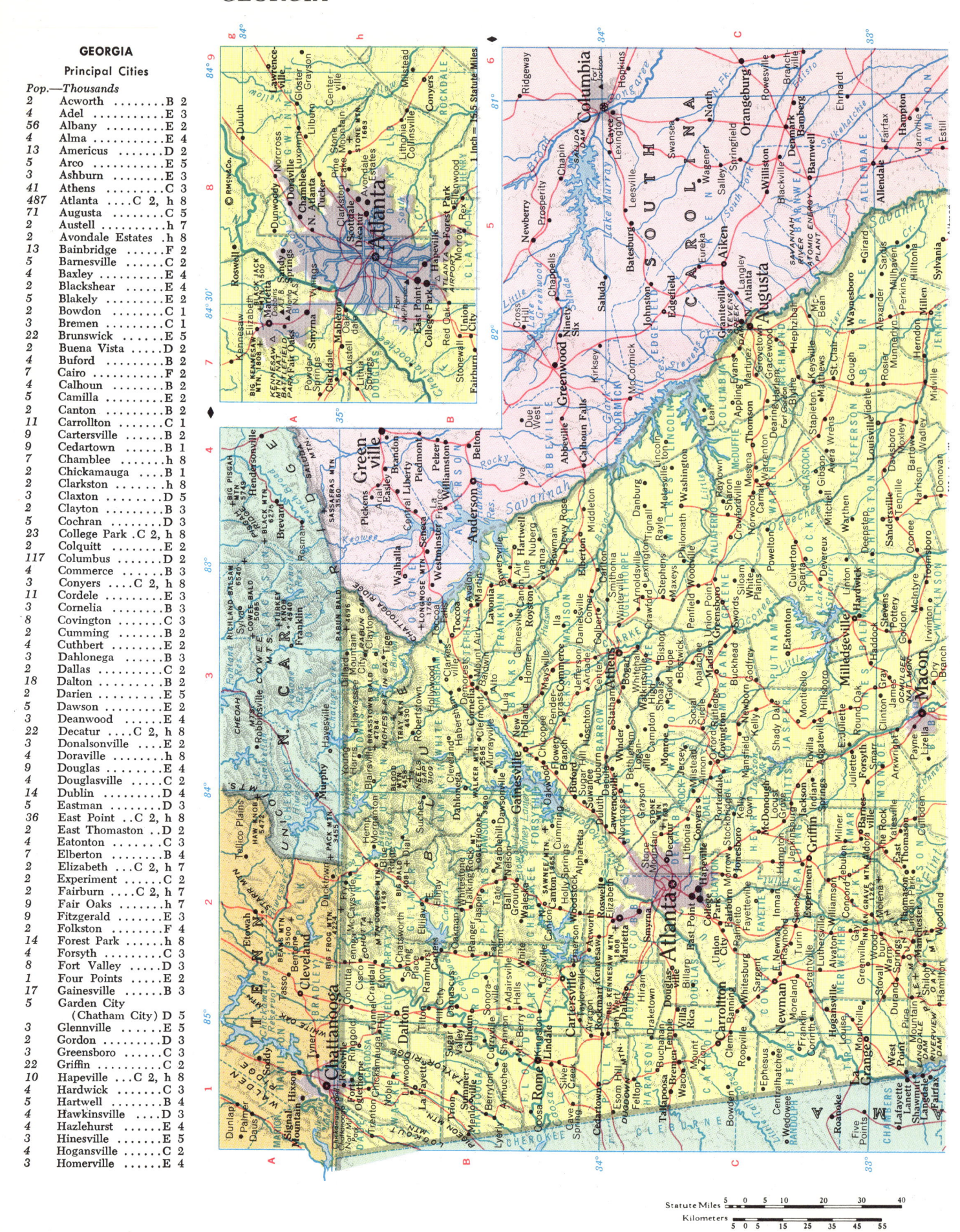

GEORGIA
Principal Cities

Pop.—Thousands		
2	Acworth	B 2
4	Adel	E 3
56	Albany	E 2
4	Alma	E 4
13	Americus	D 2
5	Arco	E 5
3	Ashburn	E 3
41	Athens	C 3
487	Atlanta	C 2, h 8
71	Augusta	C 5
2	Austell	h 7
2	Avondale Estates	h 8
13	Bainbridge	F 2
5	Barnesville	C 2
4	Baxley	E 4
2	Blackshear	E 4
5	Blakely	E 2
2	Bowdon	C 1
3	Bremen	C 1
22	Brunswick	E 5
2	Buena Vista	D 2
4	Buford	C 2
7	Cairo	F 2
4	Calhoun	B 1
5	Camilla	E 2
2	Canton	B 2
11	Carrollton	C 1
9	Cartersville	B 1
9	Cedartown	B 1
7	Chamblee	h 8
2	Chickamauga	B 1
2	Clarkston	h 8
3	Claxton	D 5
2	Clayton	B 3
5	Cochran	D 3
23	College Park	C 2, h 8
2	Colquitt	E 2
117	Columbus	D 2
3	Commerce	C 3
3	Conyers	C 2, h 8
11	Cordele	E 3
3	Cornelia	B 3
8	Covington	C 3
2	Cumming	B 2
4	Cuthbert	E 2
3	Dahlonega	B 3
2	Dallas	C 2
18	Dalton	B 2
2	Darien	E 5
5	Dawson	E 2
3	Deanwood	E 4
22	Decatur	C 2, h 8
3	Donalsonville	E 2
4	Doraville	h 8
9	Douglas	E 4
4	Douglasville	C 2
14	Dublin	D 4
5	Eastman	D 3
36	East Point	C 2, h 8
2	East Thomaston	D 2
4	Eatonton	C 3
7	Elberton	B 4
2	Elizabeth	C 2, h 7
2	Experiment	C 2
2	Fairburn	C 2, h 7
2	Fair Oaks	h 7
9	Fitzgerald	E 3
2	Folkston	F 4
14	Forest Park	h 8
4	Forsyth	C 3
8	Fort Valley	D 3
1	Four Points	E 2
17	Gainesville	B 3
5	Garden City (Chatham City)	D 5
3	Glennville	E 5
2	Gordon	D 3
3	Greensboro	C 3
22	Griffin	C 2
10	Hapeville	C 2, h 8
4	Hardwick	C 3
5	Hartwell	B 4
4	Hawkinsville	D 3
4	Hazlehurst	E 4
3	Hinesville	E 5
4	Hogansville	C 2
3	Homerville	E 4

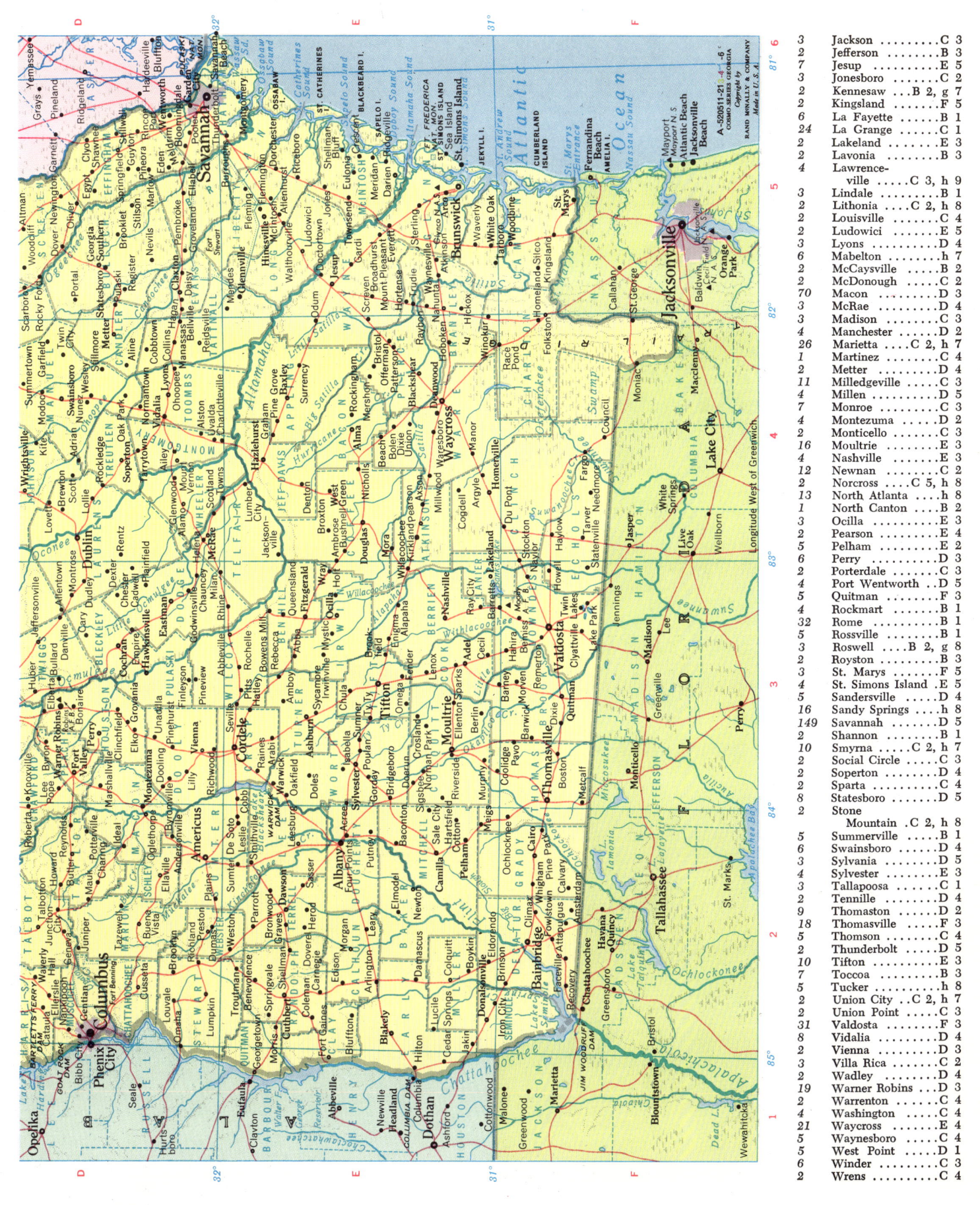

Pop.	City	Grid
3	Jackson	C 3
2	Jefferson	B 3
7	Jesup	E 5
3	Jonesboro	C 2
2	Kennesaw	B 2, g 7
2	Kingsland	F 5
6	La Fayette	B 1
24	La Grange	C 1
2	Lakeland	E 3
2	Lavonia	B 3
4	Lawrenceville	C 3, h 9
3	Lindale	B 1
2	Lithonia	C 2, h 8
2	Louisville	C 4
2	Ludowici	E 5
3	Lyons	D 4
6	Mabelton	h 7
2	McCaysville	B 2
2	McDonough	C 2
70	Macon	D 3
3	McRae	D 4
3	Madison	C 3
4	Manchester	D 2
26	Marietta	C 2, h 7
1	Martinez	C 4
2	Metter	D 4
11	Milledgeville	C 3
4	Millen	D 5
7	Monroe	C 3
2	Montezuma	D 2
2	Monticello	C 3
16	Moultrie	E 3
4	Nashville	E 3
12	Newnan	C 2
2	Norcross	C 5, h 8
13	North Atlanta	h 8
1	North Canton	B 2
3	Ocilla	E 3
2	Pearson	E 4
5	Pelham	E 2
6	Perry	D 3
2	Porterdale	C 3
4	Port Wentworth	D 5
5	Quitman	F 3
4	Rockmart	B 1
32	Rome	B 1
5	Rossville	B 1
3	Roswell	B 2, g 8
2	Royston	B 3
3	St. Marys	F 5
4	St. Simons Island	E 5
5	Sandersville	D 4
16	Sandy Springs	h 8
149	Savannah	D 5
2	Shannon	B 1
10	Smyrna	C 2, h 7
2	Social Circle	C 3
2	Soperton	D 4
2	Sparta	C 3
8	Statesboro	D 5
2	Stone Mountain	C 2, h 8
5	Summerville	B 1
6	Swainsboro	D 4
3	Sylvania	D 5
4	Sylvester	E 3
3	Tallapoosa	C 1
2	Tennille	D 4
9	Thomaston	D 2
18	Thomasville	F 3
5	Thomson	C 4
2	Thunderbolt	D 5
10	Tifton	E 3
7	Toccoa	B 3
5	Tucker	h 8
2	Union City	C 2, h 7
2	Union Point	C 3
31	Valdosta	F 3
8	Vidalia	D 4
2	Vienna	D 3
3	Villa Rica	C 2
2	Wadley	D 4
19	Warner Robins	D 3
2	Warrenton	C 4
4	Washington	C 4
21	Waycross	E 4
5	Waynesboro	C 4
5	West Point	D 1
6	Winder	C 3
2	Wrens	C 4

Lambert Conformal Conic Projection
SCALE 1:1,962,000   1 Inch = 31 Statute Miles

The Georgia of yesterday produced only cotton. Today it produces, among other things, the country's largest crop of peanuts, shown growing in the background.

GEORGIA

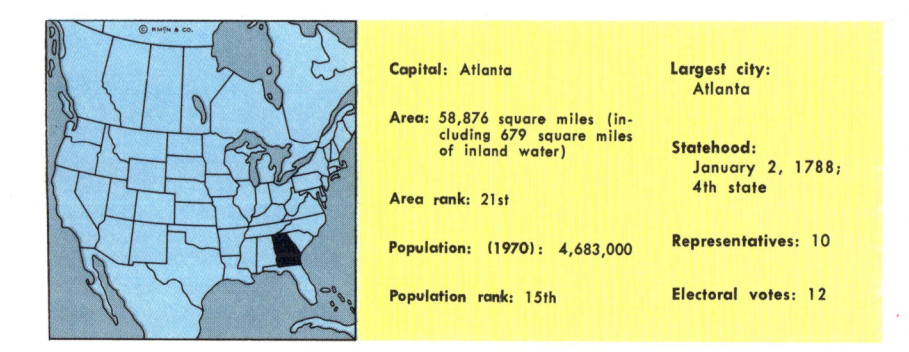

Capital: Atlanta

Area: 58,876 square miles (including 679 square miles of inland water)

Area rank: 21st

Population: (1970): 4,683,000

Population rank: 15th

Largest city: Atlanta

Statehood: January 2, 1788; 4th state

Representatives: 10

Electoral votes: 12

Along the coast of Georgia, roads seem to be half bridges and causeways, running through a sea of tall, coarse grass, and now and then crossing a stretch of open water. This coastal region is a watery land of islands, sounds, creeks, river mouths, and salt marshes. Even miles inland there are large swamps—dark, mysterious, water-filled forests, with shadowy Spanish moss draping the trees. The largest is the Okefenokee Swamp on the border of Florida.

From this low, coastal region on the southeast, Georgia rises gradually to the Appalachians in the northwest.

Georgia was last settled of the thirteen colonies. The settlement began with Savannah, founded in 1733. Georgia settlers had trouble finding a cash crop suited to their land and climate, but finally found what they needed in rice, already grown in the Carolinas. Some of the farmers grew cotton, but removal of the seeds was slow and costly. Then in 1793, Eli Whitney invented the cotton gin, a machine for removing the seeds. Cotton-growing expanded rapidly. In the twentieth century, ravages of an insect, called the boll weevil, lowered fertility of the soil because of serious erosion, and competition from increased cotton-growing in other countries combined to discourage the cotton growers. Today, old-time cotton-growers would be astonished to learn that livestock, from beef cattle to broiler chickens, now brings more income to Georgia farmers than all their crops combined.

Forests have always been a source of profit in Georgia. Early settlers began tapping the pine trees for naval stores, so-called because they were necessities on wooden sailing vessels —tar as a preservative for the ropes, pitch to calk the seams, and turpentine for paint.

Atlanta, the capital, is the largest city of Georgia. It is a transportation, wholesale, and cultural center for a large area in the eastern South.

Savannah is the principal port. A suburb of Savannah and many other small ports are the bases for fishing fleets. The offshore islands, called the Sea Islands, have many miles of beautiful sandy beaches.

HAWAII

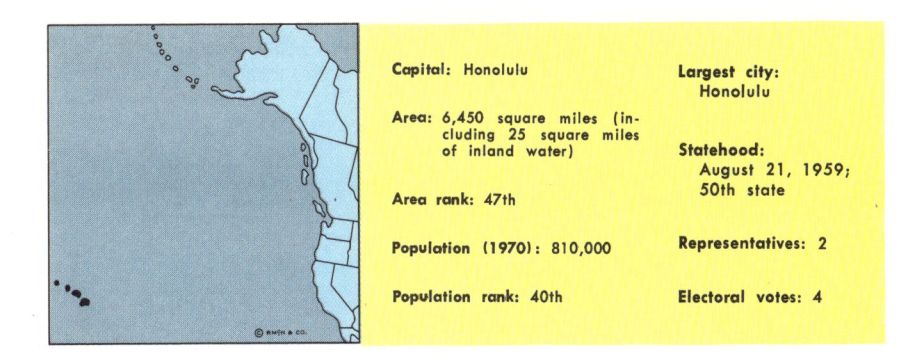

Capital: Honolulu

Area: 6,450 square miles (including 25 square miles of inland water)

Area rank: 47th

Population (1970): 810,000

Population rank: 40th

Largest city: Honolulu

Statehood: August 21, 1959; 50th state

Representatives: 2

Electoral votes: 4

Spectacular scenery, a warm climate, and beautiful beaches like palm-edged Waikiki at Honolulu, shown in this picture, have made Hawaii a favorite vacationland.

Hawaii is the fiftieth and newest state. Made up of eight large mid-Pacific islands and many tiny ones, it enjoys a delightful climate and brilliant tropical scenery. At the same time, it is an important trade, transportation, and military center.

The Hawaiian Islands, about 2,000 miles from San Francisco, are scattered across the Pacific for about 1,500 miles. The largest is Hawaii, with Maui and Oahu next in size. Honolulu, on Oahu, is the capital, and is a favorite spot for tourists.

The people of Hawaii are an unusual mixture of races and cultures, free from the frictions that often have resulted from such contacts elsewhere. Caucasians make up the largest percentage of the population, with people of Japanese ancestry somewhat fewer in numbers, and part-Hawaiians, Filipinos, and Chinese next. Pure Hawaiians now number less than two per cent, but their picturesque customs and native food, dress, and easy informality have left an indelible mark on the islands.

The economy is based chiefly on the military installations, tourism, sugar cane, and pineapples. Sugar cane has for many years been the leading agricultural product of the nation's newest state.

Pineapples are Hawaii's second most important product. The present high-grade variety, originally imported to Hawaii from Jamaica by an English resident, fills almost one-quarter of the world's demand.

The original Hawaiians were Polynesians. Europe first learned of the Hawaiians in 1778 when Captain James Cook, an Englishman, discovered the islands. Cook returned to the islands the following year, and was killed. The various islands were ruled by a number of different native chiefs at that time, but later one of them, Kamehameha, united the islands under his rule and founded a dynasty that lasted a hundred years.

The Republic of Hawaii was formed in 1894. Four years later the United States annexed the territory at the request of its people. After World War I, there was increasing desire in the islands for statehood. It was achieved in 1959.

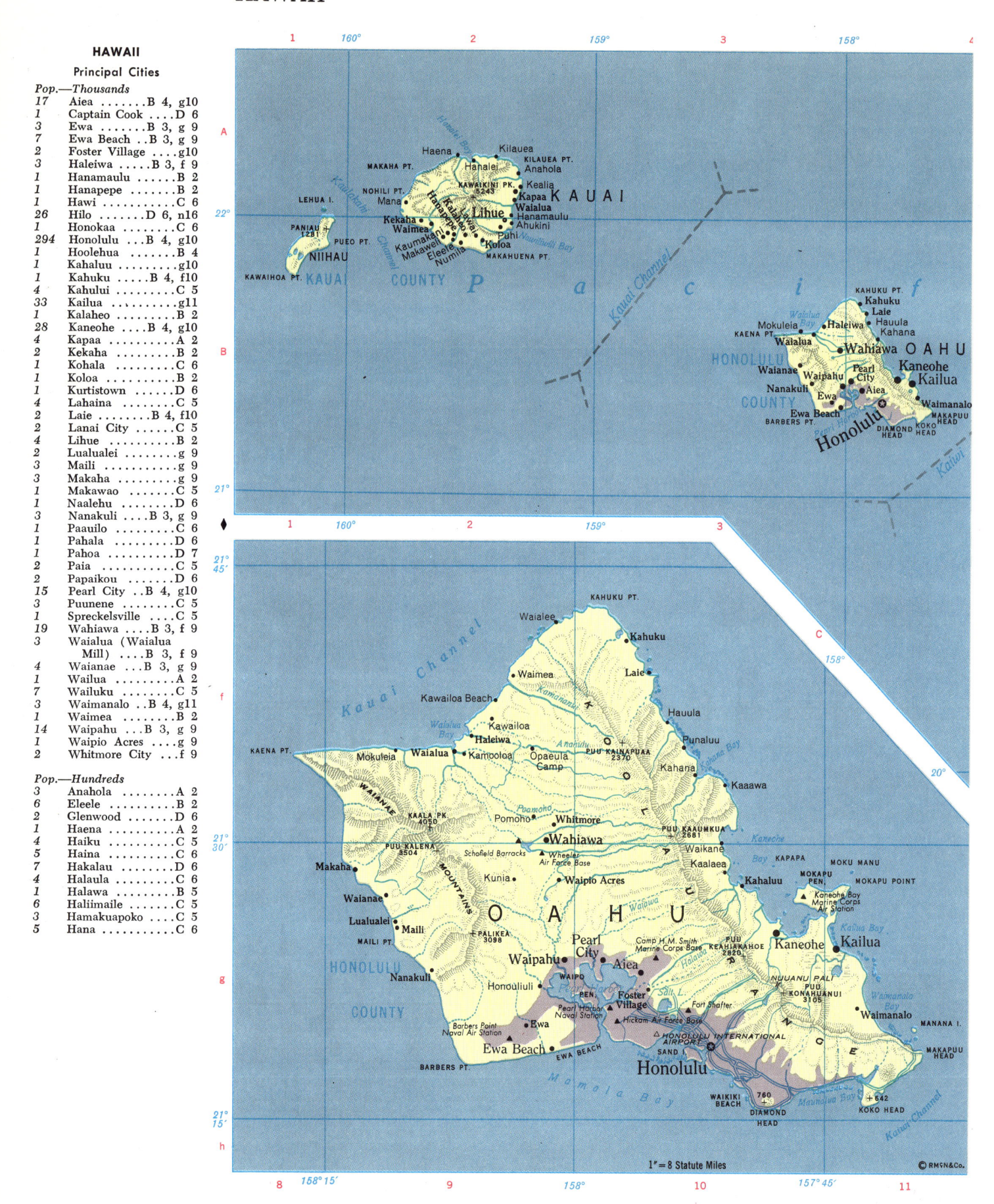

HAWAII

HAWAII
Principal Cities

Pop.—Thousands

Pop.	City	Grid
17	Aiea	B 4, g10
1	Captain Cook	D 6
3	Ewa	B 3, g 9
7	Ewa Beach	B 3, g 9
2	Foster Village	g10
3	Haleiwa	B 3, f 9
1	Hanamaulu	B 2
1	Hanapepe	B 2
1	Hawi	C 6
26	Hilo	D 6, n16
1	Honokaa	C 6
294	Honolulu	B 4, g10
1	Hoolehua	B 4
1	Kahaluu	g10
1	Kahuku	B 4, f10
4	Kahului	C 5
33	Kailua	g11
1	Kalaheo	B 2
28	Kaneohe	B 4, g10
4	Kapaa	A 2
2	Kekaha	B 2
1	Kohala	C 6
1	Koloa	B 2
1	Kurtistown	D 6
4	Lahaina	C 5
2	Laie	B 4, f10
2	Lanai City	C 5
4	Lihue	B 2
2	Lualualei	g 9
3	Maili	g 9
3	Makaha	g 9
1	Makawao	C 5
1	Naalehu	D 6
3	Nanakuli	B 3, g 9
1	Paauilo	C 6
1	Pahala	D 6
1	Pahoa	D 7
2	Paia	C 5
2	Papaikou	D 6
15	Pearl City	B 4, g10
3	Puunene	C 5
1	Spreckelsville	C 5
19	Wahiawa	B 3, f 9
3	Waialua (Waialua Mill)	B 3, f 9
4	Waianae	B 3, g 9
1	Wailua	A 2
7	Wailuku	C 5
3	Waimanalo	B 4, g11
1	Waimea	B 2
14	Waipahu	B 3, g10
1	Waipio Acres	g 9
2	Whitmore City	f 9

Pop.—Hundreds

Pop.	City	Grid
3	Anahola	A 2
6	Eleele	B 2
2	Glenwood	D 6
1	Haena	A 2
4	Haiku	C 5
5	Haina	C 5
7	Hakalau	D 6
4	Halaula	C 6
1	Halawa	B 5
6	Haliimaile	C 5
3	Hamakuapoko	C 5
5	Hana	C 6

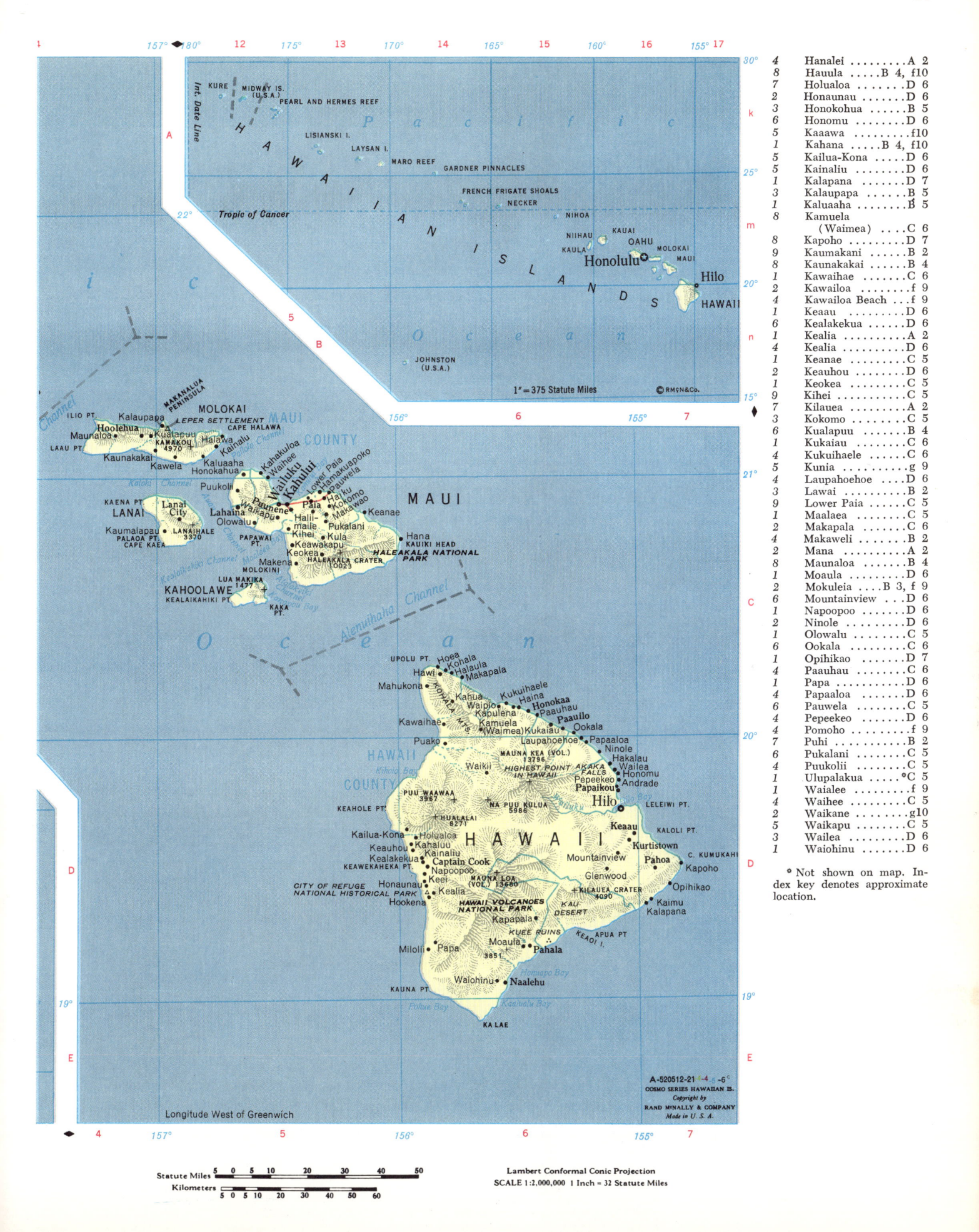

4	Hanalei	A 2
8	Hauula	B 4, f10
7	Holualoa	D 6
2	Honaunau	D 6
3	Honokohua	B 5
5	Honomu	D 6
5	Kaaawa	f10
1	Kahana	B 4, f10
5	Kailua-Kona	D 6
5	Kainaliu	D 6
1	Kalapana	D 7
3	Kalaupapa	B 5
1	Kaluaaha	B 5
8	Kamuela (Waimea)	C 6
8	Kapoho	D 7
9	Kaumakani	B 2
8	Kaunakakai	B 4
8	Kawaihae	C 6
2	Kawailoa	f 9
4	Kawailoa Beach	f 9
1	Keaau	D 6
6	Kealakekua	D 6
1	Kealia	A 2
4	Kealia	D 6
1	Keanae	C 5
2	Keauhou	D 6
5	Keokea	C 5
9	Kihei	C 5
7	Kilauea	A 2
3	Kokomo	C 5
6	Kualapuu	B 4
1	Kukaiau	C 6
4	Kukuihaele	C 6
5	Kunia	g 9
4	Laupahoehoe	D 6
3	Lawai	B 2
9	Lower Paia	C 5
1	Maalaea	C 5
4	Makapala	C 6
3	Makaweli	B 2
2	Mana	A 2
8	Maunaloa	B 4
1	Moaula	D 6
2	Mokuleia	B 3, f 9
6	Mountainview	D 6
1	Napoopoo	D 6
2	Ninole	D 6
1	Olowalu	C 5
6	Ookala	C 6
1	Opihikao	D 7
4	Paauhau	C 6
1	Papa	D 6
4	Papaaloa	D 6
6	Pauwela	C 5
4	Pepeekeo	D 6
4	Pomoho	f 9
7	Puhi	B 2
6	Pukalani	C 5
4	Puukolii	C 5
1	Ulupalakua	°C 5
1	Waialee	f 9
4	Waihee	C 5
2	Waikane	g10
5	Waikapu	C 5
3	Wailea	D 6
1	Waiohinu	D 6

° Not shown on map. Index key denotes approximate location.

Blue sky, yellow sun, and white snow attract skiers from all over to Sun Valley, in the midst of the mountains of central Idaho.

IDAHO

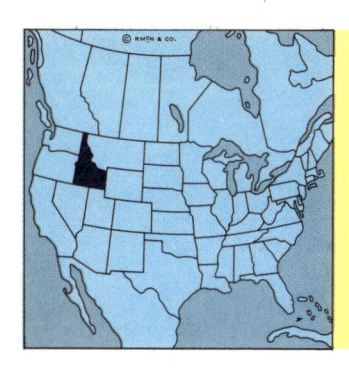

Capital: Boise

Area: 83,557 square miles (including 880 square miles of inland water)

Area rank: 13th

Population (1970): 704,000

Population rank: 42nd

Largest city: Boise

Statehood: July 3, 1890; 43rd state

Representatives: 2

Electoral votes: 4

If people in other states were asked for the first word that comes to mind when they hear the name Idaho, most of them would answer "potatoes." Idaho produces more potatoes than any other state, and the large, mealy, white Idaho baking potatoes appear on menus throughout the country.

The geography of Idaho is unusual and interesting. On a map, Idaho has a very curious shape. The southern end is a block of land with straight-line boundaries, and so is the northern end; but the southern boundary is more than 300 miles long, while the northern is less than 45. The narrowing-in occurs along the border with Montana, which follows the twisting, crooked crest of the Bitterroot Range of mountains.

Most of Idaho is a great mass of mountains; but across the wide southern section the Snake River flows in a long curve. Nearly all the level land in the state is along this river.

The Lewis and Clark Expedition of 1803–1805 found crossing the confused mass of mountains and high valleys the most difficult part of their trip. A number of later explorers lost their lives trying to go down the Snake River in boats. When they came unexpectedly upon the wild water and unscalable walls of the Snake River Canyon, it was too late to escape. The Oregon Trail followed the Snake, but left it above the canyon to cut across the steep Blue Mountains.

Most of Idaho's potatoes are grown in the wide Snake River Valley, where all the farmland must be irrigated. Sugar beets, prunes, hay, alfalfa, and red clover are grown also. Grazing land in the valley supports many cattle and sheep.

Idaho has one quite different farming region, which is partly in Washington. This is a dry-farming area around Lewiston. There is just enough moisture, without irrigation, for special crops. Two products are outstanding—wheat and dried peas. Farming in this area is large-scale and highly mechanized.

The mountains of Idaho are well forested almost to the top. Lumbering is important wherever there is adequate transportation.

Gold was discovered in Idaho in 1860, but the most valuable metal ores mined now are silver, lead, and zinc. Phosphate rock is mined also. The principal mining region is the Coeur d'Alene district in the north.

The large lumbering and milling industries of Idaho are supported by the vast forests that still cover much of the state.

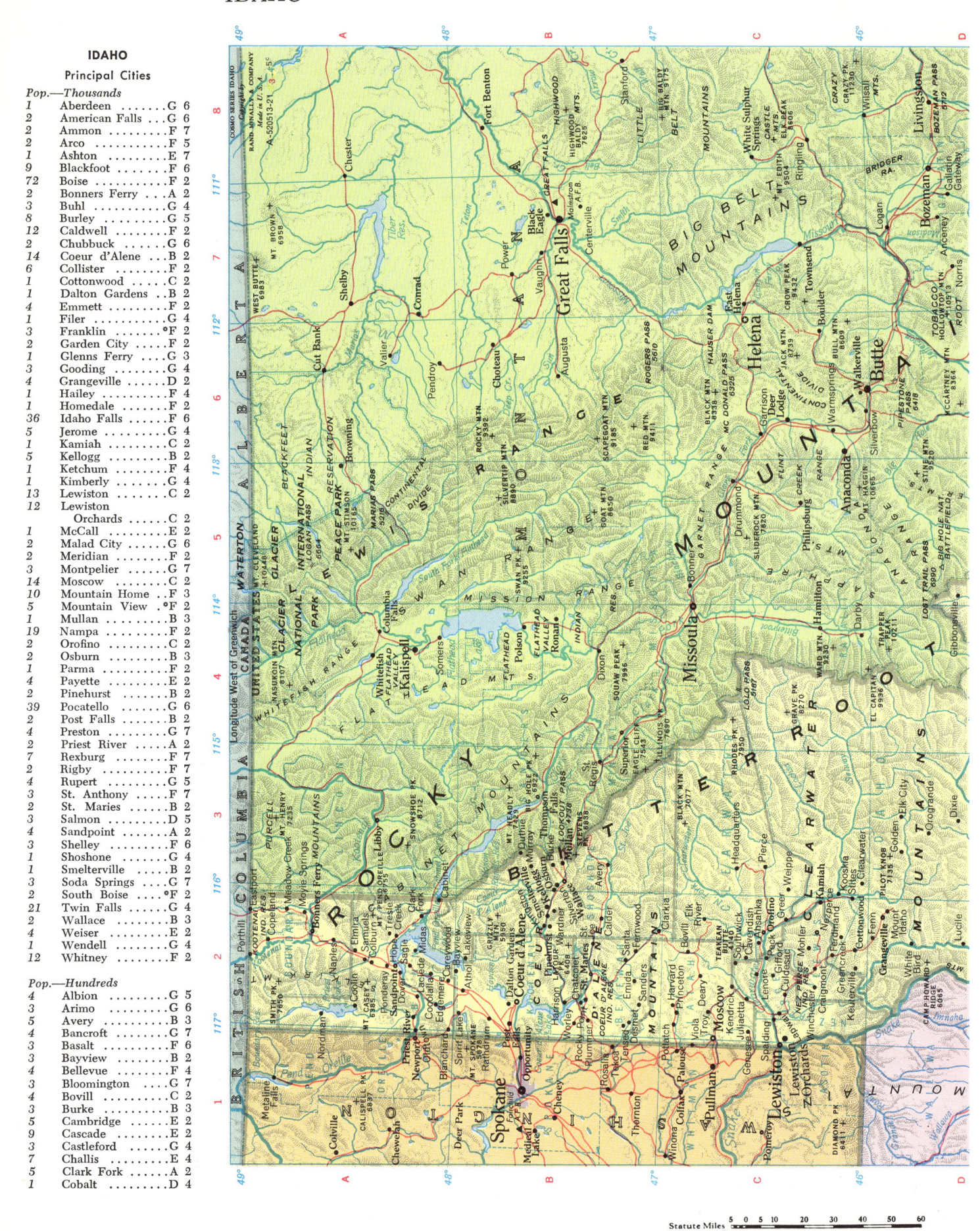

IDAHO

IDAHO
Principal Cities

Pop.—Thousands

Pop	City	Grid
1	Aberdeen	G 6
2	American Falls	G 6
2	Ammon	F 7
2	Arco	F 5
1	Ashton	E 7
9	Blackfoot	F 6
72	Boise	F 2
2	Bonners Ferry	A 2
3	Buhl	G 4
8	Burley	G 5
12	Caldwell	F 2
2	Chubbuck	G 6
14	Coeur d'Alene	B 2
6	Collister	F 2
1	Cottonwood	C 2
1	Dalton Gardens	B 2
4	Emmett	F 2
1	Filer	G 4
3	Franklin	°F 2
2	Garden City	F 2
1	Glenns Ferry	G 3
2	Gooding	G 4
4	Grangeville	D 2
1	Hailey	F 4
1	Homedale	F 2
36	Idaho Falls	F 6
5	Jerome	G 4
1	Kamiah	C 2
5	Kellogg	B 2
1	Ketchum	F 4
1	Kimberly	G 4
13	Lewiston	C 2
12	Lewiston Orchards	C 2
1	McCall	E 2
2	Malad City	G 6
2	Meridian	F 2
3	Montpelier	G 7
14	Moscow	C 2
10	Mountain Home	F 3
5	Mountain View	°F 2
1	Mullan	B 3
19	Nampa	F 2
2	Orofino	C 2
2	Osburn	B 3
1	Parma	F 2
4	Payette	E 2
2	Pinehurst	B 2
39	Pocatello	G 6
2	Post Falls	B 2
4	Preston	G 7
2	Priest River	A 2
7	Rexburg	F 7
2	Rigby	F 7
4	Rupert	G 5
3	St. Anthony	F 7
2	St. Maries	B 2
3	Salmon	D 5
4	Sandpoint	A 2
3	Shelley	F 6
1	Shoshone	G 4
1	Smelterville	B 2
3	Soda Springs	G 7
2	South Boise	°F 2
21	Twin Falls	G 4
2	Wallace	B 3
4	Weiser	E 2
1	Wendell	G 4
12	Whitney	F 2

Pop.—Hundreds

Pop	City	Grid
4	Albion	G 5
3	Arimo	G 6
5	Avery	B 3
4	Bancroft	G 7
3	Basalt	F 6
3	Bayview	B 2
4	Bellevue	F 4
3	Bloomington	G 7
4	Bovill	C 2
3	Burke	B 3
5	Cambridge	E 2
9	Cascade	E 2
3	Castleford	G 4
7	Challis	E 4
5	Clark Fork	A 2
1	Cobalt	D 4

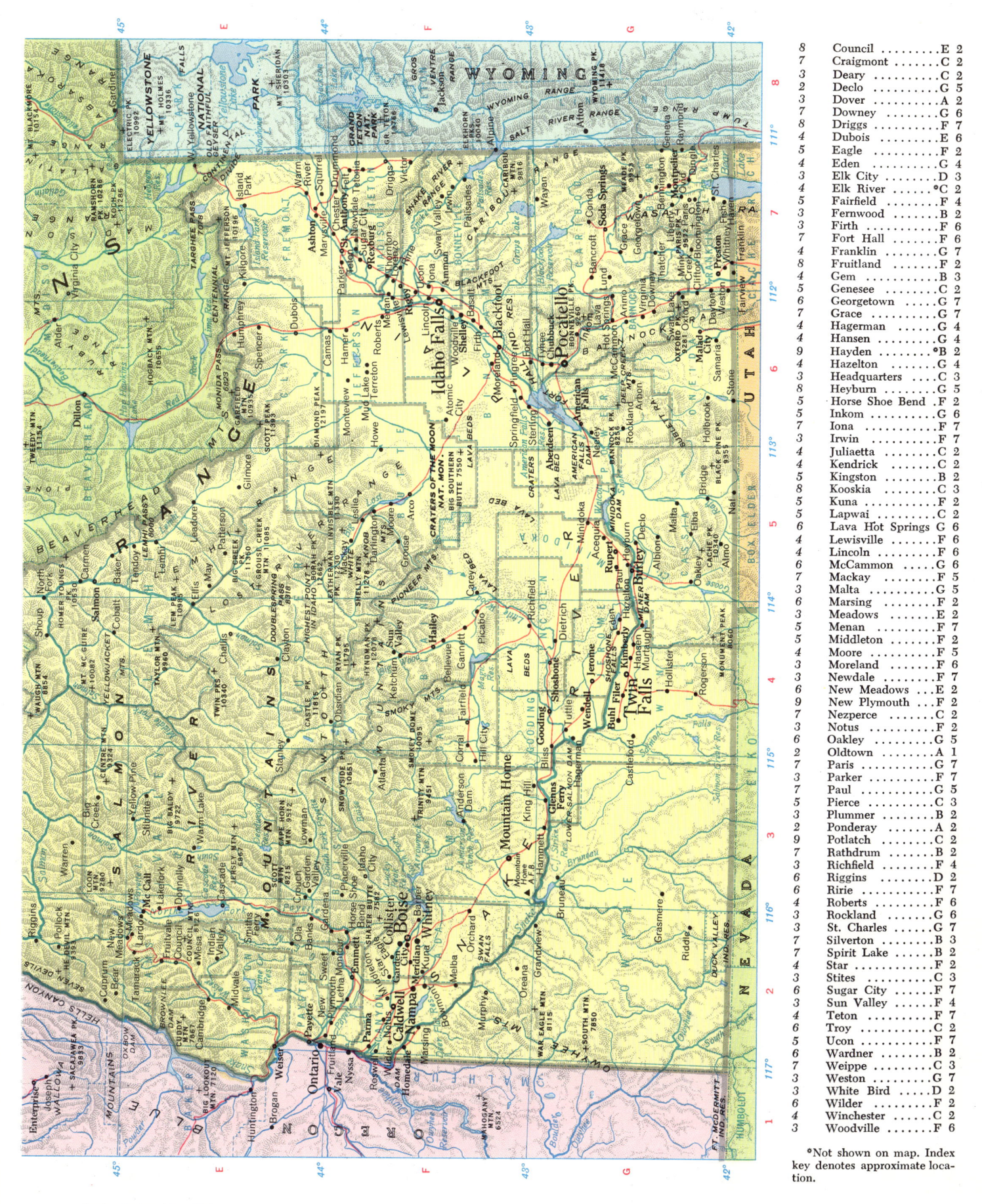

Pop	Place	Grid
8	Council	E 2
7	Craigmont	C 2
3	Deary	C 2
2	Declo	G 5
3	Dover	A 2
7	Downey	G 6
8	Driggs	F 7
4	Dubois	E 6
3	Eagle	F 2
4	Eden	G 4
3	Elk City	D 3
4	Elk River	°C 2
7	Fairfield	F 4
3	Fernwood	B 2
3	Firth	F 6
7	Fort Hall	F 6
4	Franklin	G 7
8	Fruitland	F 2
4	Gem	B 3
5	Genesee	C 2
6	Georgetown	G 7
7	Grace	G 7
4	Hagerman	G 4
4	Hansen	G 4
9	Hayden	°B 2
4	Hazelton	G 4
8	Headquarters	C 3
5	Heyburn	G 5
5	Horse Shoe Bend	F 2
5	Inkom	G 6
7	Iona	F 7
7	Irwin	F 7
4	Juliaetta	C 2
4	Kendrick	C 2
5	Kingston	B 2
4	Kooskia	C 3
5	Kuna	F 2
5	Lapwai	C 2
7	Lava Hot Springs	G 6
4	Lewisville	F 7
3	Lincoln	F 6
6	McCammon	G 6
7	Mackay	F 5
4	Malta	G 5
5	Marsing	F 2
3	Meadows	E 2
5	Menan	F 7
4	Middleton	F 2
4	Moore	F 5
5	Moreland	F 6
3	Newdale	F 7
3	New Meadows	E 2
9	New Plymouth	F 2
7	Nezperce	C 2
3	Notus	F 2
6	Oakley	G 5
2	Oldtown	A 1
7	Paris	G 7
3	Parker	F 7
5	Paul	G 5
7	Pierce	C 3
3	Plummer	B 2
3	Ponderay	A 2
7	Potlatch	C 2
7	Rathdrum	B 2
6	Richfield	F 4
6	Riggins	D 2
6	Ririe	F 7
7	Roberts	F 6
4	Rockland	G 6
7	St. Charles	G 7
7	Silverton	B 3
7	Spirit Lake	B 2
3	Star	F 2
3	Stites	C 3
6	Sugar City	F 7
3	Sun Valley	F 4
4	Teton	F 7
2	Troy	C 2
5	Ucon	F 7
6	Wardner	B 2
7	Weippe	C 3
6	Weston	G 7
3	White Bird	D 2
6	Wilder	F 2
4	Winchester	C 2
3	Woodville	F 6

°Not shown on map. Index key denotes approximate location.

Lambert Conformal Conic Projection
SCALE 1:2,633,000 1 Inch = 41.5 Statute Miles

ILLINOIS

ILLINOIS
Principal Cities

Pop.—Thousands

Pop	City	Ref
20	Addison	k 8
43	Alton	E 3
53	Arlington Heights	A 5, h 9
64	Aurora	B 5, k 8
8	Barrington	A 5, h 8
7	Bartonville	C 4
8	Batavia	B 5, k 8
41	Belleville	E 4
23	Bellwood	k 9
13	Belvidere	A 5
12	Bensenville	B 6, k 9
7	Benton	E 5
54	Berwyn	k 9
38	Bloomington	C 4
22	Blue Island	B 6, k 9
9	Bradley	B 6
20	Brookfield	k 9
16	Cahokia	E 3
9	Cairo	F 4
30	Calumet City	B 6, k 9
14	Canton	C 3
19	Carbondale	F 4
23	Carpentersville	A 5, h 8
14	Centralia	E 4
13	Centreville	E 3
50	Champaign	C 5
14	Charleston	D 5
3,550	Chicago	B 6, k 9
39	Chicago Heights	B 6, k 9
69	Cicero	B 6, k 9
6	Clarendon Hills	k 9
7	Clinton	C 5
14	Collinsville	E 4
7	Creve Coeur	C 4
12	Crystal Lake	A 5, h 8
42	Danville	C 6
78	Decatur	D 5
17	Deerfield	h 9
29	De Kalb	B 5
57	Des Plaines	A 6, h 9
20	Dixon	B 4
24	Dolton	k 9
26	Downers Grove	B 5, k 8
8	East Alton	E 3
21	East Moline	B 3
17	East Peoria	C 4
82	East St. Louis	E 3
11	Edwardsville	E 4
8	Effingham	D 5
49	Elgin	A 5, h 8
17	Elk Grove Village	h 8
46	Elmhurst	B 6, k 9
24	Elmwood Park	k 9
79	Evanston	A 6, h 9
27	Evergreen Park	k 9
15	Forest Park	k 9
20	Franklin Park	k 9
27	Freeport	A 4
37	Galesburg	C 3
9	Geneva	B 5, k 8
10	Glencoe	A 6, h 9
21	Glen Ellyn	k 8
24	Glenview	h 9
40	Granite City	E 3
33	Harvey	B 6, k 9
9	Hazel Crest	k 9
10	Herrin	F 4
33	Highland Park	A 6, h 9
15	Hinsdale	k 9
19	Homewood	B 6, k 9
7	Hoopeston	C 6
22	Jacksonville	D 3
67	Joliet	B 5, k 8
31	Kankakee	B 6
16	Kewanee	B 4
16	La Grange	B 6, k 9
15	La Grange Park	k 9
13	Lake Forest	A 6, h 9
23	Lansing	B 6, k 9
12	La Salle	B 4
11	Libertyville	A 6, h 9
17	Lincoln	C 4
14	Lincolnwood	h 9

7	Litchfield	D 4
9	Lockport	B 5, k 8
31	Lombard	k 8
11	Loves Park	A 4
11	Lyons	k 9
19	Macomb	C 3
7	Madison	E 5
11	Marion	F 5
19	Markham	k 9
19	Mattoon	D 5
29	Maywood	k 9
22	Melrose Park	k 9
7	Mendota	B 4
12	Midlothian	k 9
43	Moline	B 3
10	Monmouth	C 3
8	Morris	B 5
10	Morton	C 4
27	Morton Grove	h 9
30	Mount Carmel	E 6
30	Mount Prospect	A 6, h 9
16	Mount Vernon	E 5
16	Mundelein	A 5, h 9
55	Murphysboro	F 4
19	Naperville	B 5, k 8
32	Niles	h 9
17	Normal	C 5
17	Norridge	k 9
23	Northbrook	h 9
	North Chicago	A 6, h 9
14	Northlake	k 9
15	North Park	A 4
10	Oak Lawn	B 6, k 9
62	Oak Park	B 6, k 9
9	Olney	E 5
19	Ottawa	B 5
24	Palatine	A 5, h 8
10	Paris	D 6
31	Park Forest	B 6, m 9
40	Park Ridge	B 6, h 9
29	Pekin	C 4
103	Peoria	C 4
7	Peoria Heights	C 4
8	Peru	B 4
7	Pontiac	C 5
8	Princeton	B 4
44	Quincy	D 2
28	Rantoul	C 5
16	Riverdale	k 9
13	River Forest	k 9
11	River Grove	k 9
10	Riverside	k 9
8	Robbins	k 9
10	Rochelle	B 4
10	Rock Falls	B 4
132	Rockford	A 4
52	Rock Island	B 3
18	Rolling Meadows	h 8
11	St. Charles	B 5, k 8
6	Salem	E 5
11	Schiller Park	k 9
5	Shelbyville	D 5
70	Skokie	A 6, h 9
21	South Holland	k 9
25	South Stickney	k 9
83	Springfield	D 4
6	Steger	B 6, m 9
16	Sterling	B 4
17	Streator	B 5
10	Summit	k 9
7	Sycamore	B 5
9	Taylorville	D 4
9	Tinley Park	k 9
27	Urbana	C 5
6	Vandalia	E 4
26	Villa Park	k 8
7	Washington Park	E 3
56	Waukegan	A 6, h 9
18	Westchester	k 9
8	West Chicago	k 8
13	Western Springs	k 9
9	West Frankfort	F 5
6	Westmont	k 9
28	Wheaton	B 5, k 8
14	Wheeling	h 9
32	Wilmette	A 6, h 9
13	Winnetka	A 6, h 9
12	Wood River	E 3
10	Woodstock	A 5
12	Worth	k 9
14	Zion	A 6, h 9

Lambert Conformal Conic Projection
SCALE 1:1,997,000   1 Inch = 31.5 Statute Miles

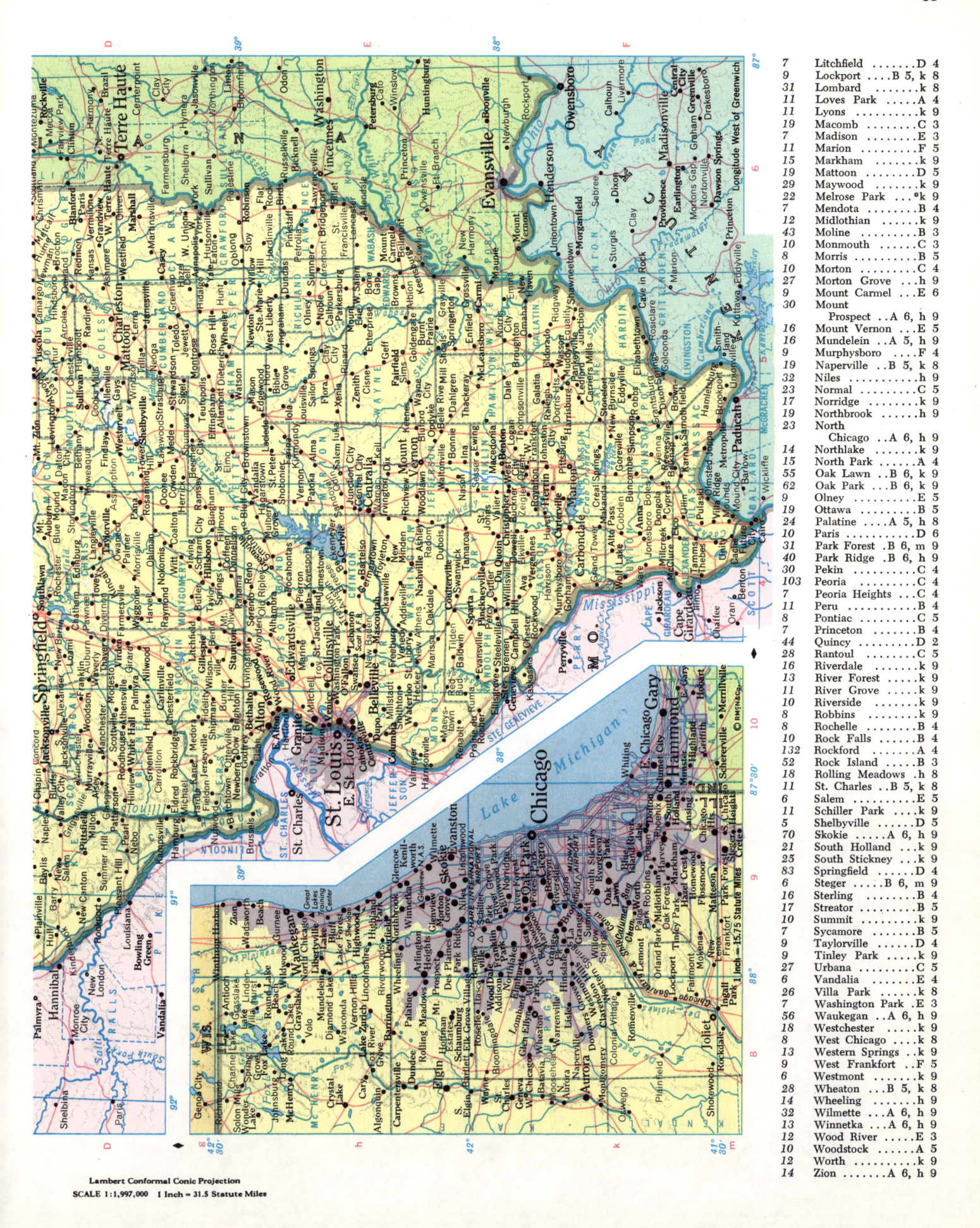

ILLINOIS

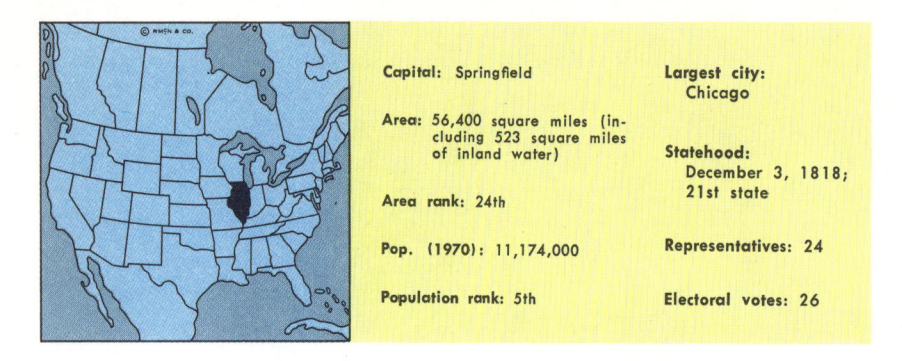

Capital: Springfield

Area: 56,400 square miles (including 523 square miles of inland water)

Area rank: 24th

Pop. (1970): 11,174,000

Population rank: 5th

Largest city: Chicago

Statehood: December 3, 1818; 21st state

Representatives: 24

Electoral votes: 26

Illinois belongs to the great industrial region that occupies the northeastern quarter of the United States. It is also a corn-belt state, a livestock-feeding state, a Mississippi River State, and a Great Lakes state. It is a heavy producer of corn, hogs, beef cattle, soybeans, and fruit, although over 60 per cent of its people live in the metropolitan area of Chicago, one of the three largest cities in the United States.

The name of Illinois reflects two phases of its early background, Indian and French. Both the state and its longest river were named for an Indian tribe called the Illini. As the present spelling of the word suggests, the first Europeans to write it were French. The Illinois country was first explored by Father Marquette and Louis Joliet in 1673. LaSalle followed a little later and claimed the whole center of the present United States for France, and it remained French until 1763. A few French settlers came to the present southern Illinois.

Real settlement took place in the early 1800's. Most of the very early settlers came down the Ohio River. A little later many came overland by way of the National Road, which ended at Vandalia. The people who came by these routes settled mainly in southern Illinois and gave it a large enough population to be admitted as a state in 1818. A second wave of settlers came to the northern part of the state by way of the Great Lakes.

Chicago owes its growth largely to its location on Lake Michigan, at a point within the great agricultural and industrial heart of the country. The St. Lawrence Seaway has made it a greater shipping center than ever, but from pioneer times Chicago has been a leading Great Lakes port.

After the coming of the railways Chicago became a great rail center, because many lines met there since rail traffic had either to pass around the southern end of Lake Michigan or cross into Canada to the north. Later, Chicago became a great highway center, and with the beginning of commercial flying, it also became a great air center. Its location on Lake Michigan has helped make it a beautiful, as well as an industrial city. Its Outer Drive, a boulevard that runs for miles along the lake front through parks and past beaches, yacht harbors, and museums, is one of the most beautiful metropolitan roadways in the country.

Chicago's magnificent skyline sparkles brilliantly against the night-time darkness of the Mid-American sky.

Fertile fields, ponds, and sheltering trees around prosperous farms make much of Illinois an ideal picture of rural America.

INDIANA

INDIANA
Principal Cities

Pop.—Thousands	City	Grid
2	Albany	D 7
6	Alexandria	D 6
70	Anderson	D 6
5	Angola	A 8
4	Attica	D 3
7	Auburn	B 7
5	Aurora	F 8
5	Austin	G 6
3	Batesville	F 7
13	Bedford	G 5
13	Beech Grove	E 5, m10
3	Berne	C 8
4	Bicknell	G 3
2	Boomfield	F 4
42	Bloomington	F 4
6	Bluffton	C 7
5	Boonville	H 3
2	Bourbon	B 5
9	Brazil	E 3
2	Bremen	B 5
3	Brookville	F 8
5	Brownsburg	E 5
2	Brownstown	G 5
2	Butler	B 8
3	Cambridge City	E 7
2	Cannelton	I 4
7	Cedar Lake	A 3
2	Centerville	E 8
2	Chandler	H 3
6	Charlestown	H 6
3	Chesterfield	D 6
5	Chesterton	A 3
9	Clarksville	H 6
6	Clinton	E 3
5	Columbia City	B 7
25	Columbus	F 6
18	Connersville	E 7
3	Corydon	H 5
3	Covington	D 3
14	Crawfordsville	D 4
10	Crown Point	B 3
2	Culver	B 5
2	Daleville	D 6
3	Danville	E 4
8	Decatur	C 8
3	Delphi	C 4
3	Dunkirk	D 7
2	Dunlap	A 6
4	Dyer	B 2
58	East Chicago	A 3
9	East Gary	A 3
2	Eaton	D 7
4	Edinburg	F 6
40	Elkhart	A 6
12	Elwood	D 6
142	Evansville	I 2
3	Fairmount	D 6
2	Flora	C 4
2	Fort Branch	H 2
2	Fortville	E 6
173	Fort Wayne	B 7
3	Fowler	C 3
15	Frankfort	D 4
11	Franklin	F 5
2	French Lick	G 4
5	Garrett	B 7
178	Gary	A 3
5	Gas City	D 6
14	Goshen	A 6
9	Greencastle	E 4
3	Greendale	F 8
9	Greenfield	E 6
7	Greensburg	F 7
11	Greenwood	E 5, m10
16	Griffith	A 3
2	Hagerstown	E 7
112	Hammond	A 2
8	Hartford City	D 7
23	Highland	A 3
21	Hobart	A 3
4	Huntingburg	H 4
16	Huntington	C 7
476	Indianapolis	E 5, k10
2	Jasonville	F 3
8	Jasper	H 4
20	Jeffersonville	H 6
2	Jonesboro	D 6
7	Kendallville	B 7

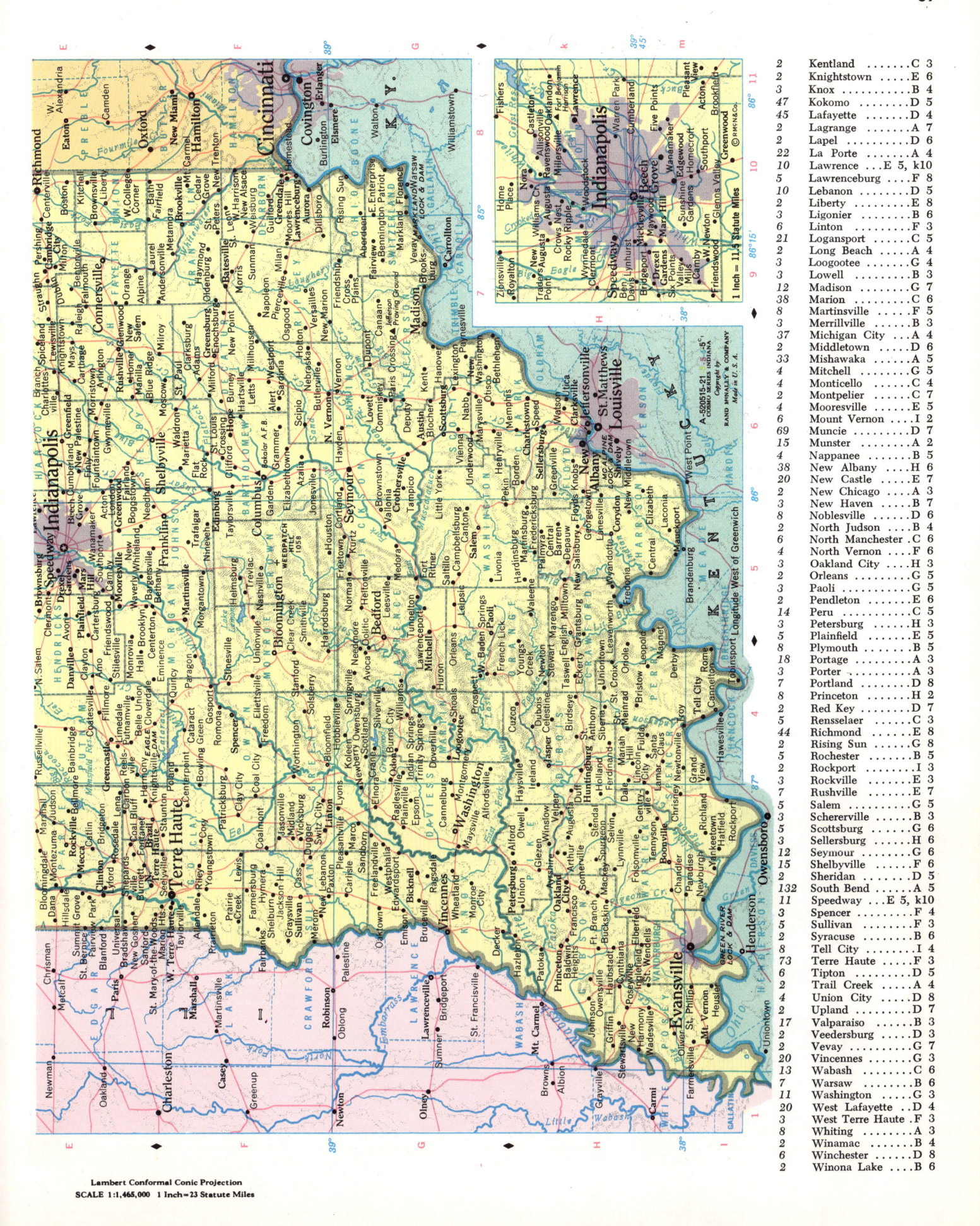

Pop.	City	Grid
2	Kentland	C 3
2	Knightstown	E 6
3	Knox	B 4
47	Kokomo	D 5
45	Lafayette	D 4
2	Lagrange	A 7
2	Lapel	D 6
22	La Porte	A 4
10	Lawrence	E 5, k10
5	Lawrenceburg	F 8
10	Lebanon	D 5
2	Liberty	E 8
3	Ligonier	B 6
6	Linton	F 3
21	Logansport	C 5
3	Long Beach	A 4
3	Loogootee	G 4
3	Lowell	B 3
12	Madison	G 7
38	Marion	C 6
8	Martinsville	D 5
3	Merrillville	B 3
37	Michigan City	A 4
2	Middletown	D 6
33	Mishawaka	A 5
4	Mitchell	G 5
4	Monticello	C 4
2	Montpelier	C 7
4	Mooresville	D 5
6	Mount Vernon	I 2
69	Muncie	D 7
15	Munster	A 2
4	Nappanee	B 5
38	New Albany	H 6
20	New Castle	E 7
2	New Chicago	A 3
4	New Haven	C 7
8	Noblesville	D 6
2	North Judson	B 4
6	North Manchester	C 6
4	North Vernon	F 6
2	Oakland City	H 3
2	Orleans	G 5
3	Paoli	G 5
2	Pendleton	E 6
14	Peru	C 5
3	Petersburg	H 3
5	Plainfield	E 5
8	Plymouth	B 5
18	Portage	A 3
3	Porter	A 3
7	Portland	D 8
7	Princeton	H 2
2	Red Key	D 7
5	Rensselaer	C 3
44	Richmond	E 8
2	Rising Sun	G 8
5	Rochester	B 5
2	Rockport	I 3
3	Rockville	E 3
5	Rushville	E 7
5	Salem	G 5
3	Schererville	B 3
3	Scottsburg	G 6
3	Sellersburg	H 6
15	Seymour	F 6
12	Shelbyville	F 6
2	Sheridan	D 5
132	South Bend	A 5
11	Speedway	E 5, k10
3	Spencer	F 4
5	Sullivan	F 3
3	Syracuse	B 6
2	Tell City	I 4
73	Terre Haute	F 3
6	Tipton	D 5
4	Trail Creek	A 4
4	Union City	D 8
3	Upland	D 7
17	Valparaiso	B 3
3	Veedersburg	D 3
2	Vevay	G 7
20	Vincennes	G 2
13	Wabash	C 6
8	Warsaw	B 6
7	Washington	G 3
20	West Lafayette	D 4
2	West Terre Haute	F 3
8	Whiting	A 3
2	Winamac	B 4
6	Winchester	D 8
2	Winona Lake	B 6

INDIANA

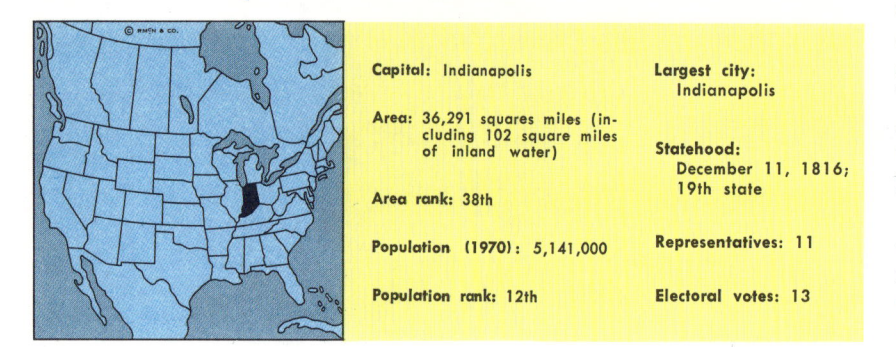

Capital: Indianapolis

Area: 36,291 squares miles (including 102 square miles of inland water)

Area rank: 38th

Population (1970): 5,141,000

Population rank: 12th

Largest city: Indianapolis

Statehood: December 11, 1816; 19th state

Representatives: 11

Electoral votes: 13

Gary, Indiana, has become one of the world's great steel-making cities, and its huge blast furnaces have provided the nation with steel needed in building and defense.

Indiana has only a narrow "window" on any of the Great Lakes—a 51-mile strip on Lake Michigan. The Calumet area, one of the great steel-production areas of the world, occupies part of it. The remainder is a great recreational area, with 25 miles of sand dunes and beaches, including the three-and-a-half mile long Dunes State Park.

Gary is the hub of the Calumet industrial area, which includes Hammond, East Chicago, and Whiting. Gary did not exist in 1905, when U.S. Steel decided to build its mills on the shores of Lake Michigan. Engineers pumped sand from the lake and spread it over 8,000 acres of dunes and swamps. On this new land, they built an $85,000,000 steel plant. Then, they filled another 7,000 acres of land and built a city named for Elbridge H. Gary of U.S. Steel. There are oil refineries and cracking plants and many other industries in the area, as well as steel mills.

The Calumet area, and the manufacturing cities of Indianapolis, Fort Wayne, South Bend, and Evansville give Indiana high rank among the states in value of manufactures.

Backing the state's manufacturing industries is a flourishing agricultural economy. From the level Corn Belt plains in the central section, the rounded hills of the south, and the lowlands of the northern lake region, the state has built a diversified agriculture. It consists of stock raising, dairy farming, and the growing of corn, soybeans, tomatoes, onions, and other vegetables. The muck soils of the north produce important supplies of peppermint and spearmint oils.

Indianapolis, the largest city, owes much of its prosperity to the state's productive land. It is a leading corn and livestock market and the trading center for a rich farming territory. The city is a major transportation center, and is widely known as the site of the Memorial Day auto race.

The Territory of Indiana was formed in 1800 from the Northwest Territory. After the defeat of powerful Indian forces by Gen. William H. Harrison at Tippecanoe in 1811, settlement of Indiana moved ahead rapidly, and statehood was achieved five years later.

IOWA

Capital: Des Moines

Area: 56,290 square miles (including 247 square miles of inland water)

Area rank: 25th

Population (1970): 2,789,000

Population rank: 25th

Largest city: Des Moines

Statehood: December 28, 1846; 29th state

Representatives: 7

Electoral votes: 9

Iowa is bounded by two mighty rivers: on the east the Mississippi, and on the west, the Missouri. At each side of the state, steep bluffs rise along the rivers. Except for the valleys of the Des Moines River and a few smaller streams, the rest of the land is gently rolling, without sharp differences in elevation. There are no large useless areas of rough country or marsh, and more than 90 per cent of the land is in farms.

Winters are quite cold, but the growing season is more than five months long and summers are hot.

Iowans boast about the height of the corn in their state, and say they live out where the tall corn grows, but the amount is more important than the height—Iowa produces more corn, as grain, than any other state. Farmers use most of the corn as feed for livestock, and it is no coincidence that Iowa also produces more hogs than any other state, or that meat-packing is a leading industry. Beef cattle come next to hogs as consumers of corn. Iowa farmers also own a great many dairy cows, sheep, and chickens.

The most beautiful scenes in the state are its rolling green pastures, broken here and there by clumps of trees, where the cows and sheep graze. Hay for the animals ranks third in value among the state's crops, and soybeans, rye, and oats are also grown as feed.

The population of Iowa is not very dense, and the largest city, Des Moines, has fewer than a quarter of a million people. The Sac and Fox, the only Indians still living in Iowa, hold land in Tama County, where they hold a large powwow each summer. The Amana Colonies, near Iowa City, were built and settled by a religious group that originated in Germany. They are still known for their fine, hearty cooking and their handicrafts, though they also have a large freezer and air conditioning equipment plant.

Iowa came to the United States as part of the Louisiana Purchase in 1803, when it was still Indian country. The first town was Dubuque, founded in 1833. Iowa won statehood in 1846. Settlement began near the Mississippi River and advanced westward. An Indian massacre near Spirit Lake temporarily stalled settlement in that area, but Iowa grew rapidly in the 1870's, after railroads had been built to meet the Union Pacific at Council Bluffs.

Iowa-bred hogs feed on Iowa-grown corn. The sharper the appetite today, the more delicious tomorrow's ham and bacon will be.

IOWA

IOWA
Principal Cities

Pop.—Thousands		
2	Ackley	B 4
2	Adel	C 3
1	Akron	B 1
5	Albia	C 5
6	Algoma	A 3
1	Altoona	C 4, e 9
35	Ames	B 4
5	Anamosa	B 6
1	Anita	C 3
3	Ankeny	A 7, C 4
7	Atlantic	C 2
3	Audubon	C 3
2	Avoca	C 2
2	Bedford	D 3
3	Belle Plaine	C 5
2	Bellevue	B 7
3	Belmond	B 4
17	Bettendorf	C 7, g11
3	Bloomfield	D 5
12	Boone	B 4
33	Burlington	D 6
3	Camanche	C 7
2	Carlisle	C 4, f 9
8	Carroll	B 3
2	Carter Lake	C 2
2	Cascade	B 6
26	Cedar Falls	B 5
104	Cedar Rapids	C 6
7	Centerville	D 5
5	Chariton	D 4
10	Charles City	A 5
8	Cherokee	B 2
6	Clarinda	D 2
3	Clarion	B 4
1	Clarksville	B 5
6	Clear Lake	A 4
34	Clinton	C 7
2	Colfax	C 4
2	Coon Rapids	C 3
3	Coralville	C 6
2	Corning	D 3
2	Corydon	D 4
53	Council Bluffs	C 2
4	Cresco	A 5
8	Creston	C 3
96	Davenport	C 7, g10
7	Decorah	A 6
7	Denison	B 2
207	Des Moines	C 4, e 8
4	De Witt	C 7
63	Dubuque	B 7
1	Dunlap	C 2
1	Durant	C 7
3	Dyersville	B 6
4	Eagle Grove	B 4
1	Eldon	D 5
3	Eldora	B 4
2	Elkader	B 6
4	Emmetsburg	A 3
8	Estherville	A 3
6	Evansdale	B 5
12	Fairfield	D 6
2	Fayette	B 6
3	Forest City	A 4
30	Fort Dodge	B 3
15	Fort Madison	D 6
2	Garner	A 4
1	George	A 2
5	Glenwood	C 2
1	Greene	B 5
2	Greenfield	C 3
8	Grinnell	C 5
2	Grundy Center	B 5
2	Guthrie Center	C 3
2	Guttenberg	B 6
2	Hamburg	D 2
5	Hampton	B 4
5	Harlan	C 2
2	Hartley	A 2
3	Hawarden	A 1
1	Hull	A 1
4	Humboldt	B 3
2	Ida Grove	B 2
5	Independence	B 6
7	Indianola	C 4
40	Iowa City	C 6
6	Iowa Falls	B 4
5	Jefferson	B 3
2	Jesup	B 5

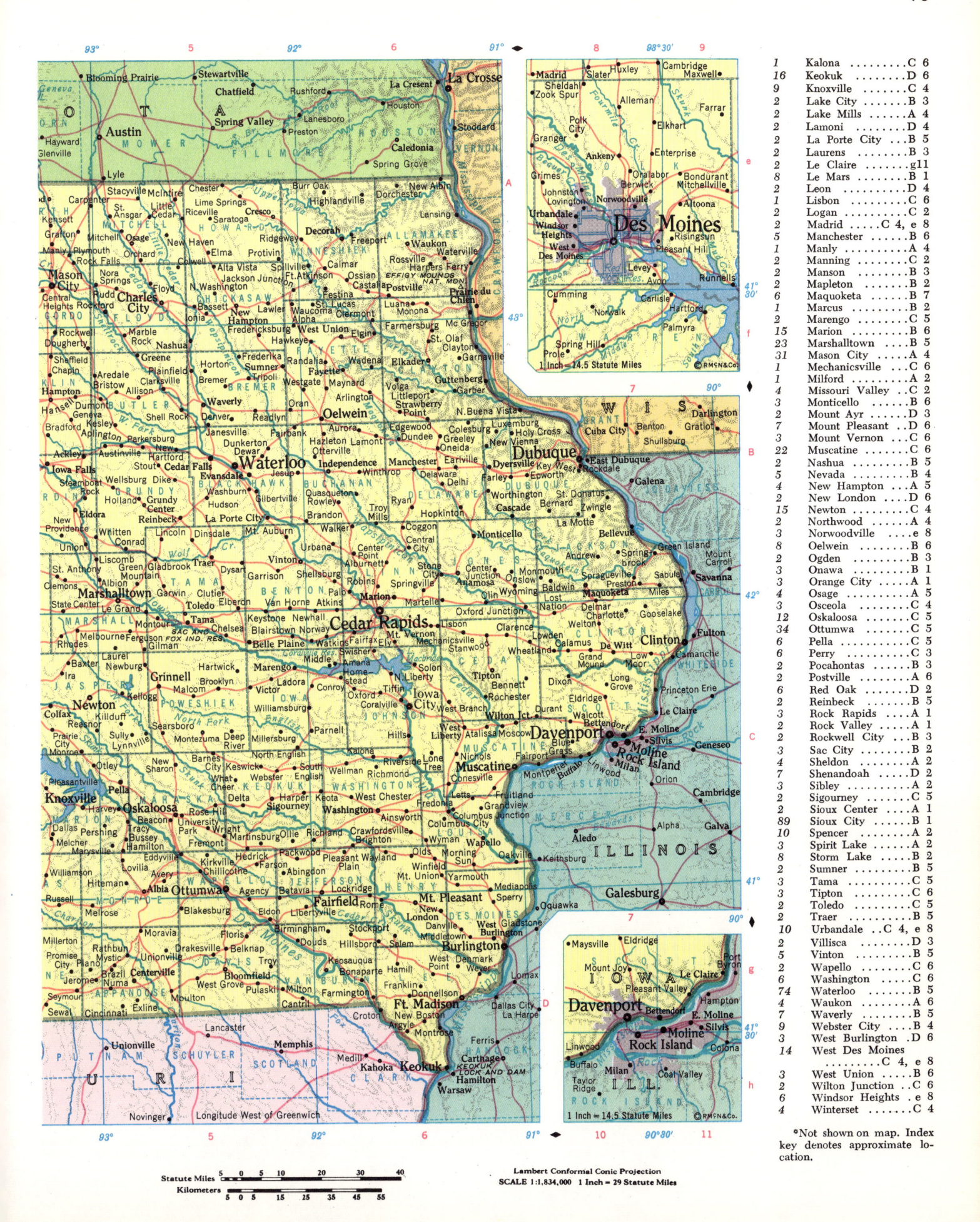

#	Place	Ref
1	Kalona	C 6
16	Keokuk	D 6
9	Knoxville	C 4
2	Lake City	B 3
2	Lake Mills	A 4
2	Lamoni	D 4
2	La Porte City	B 5
2	Laurens	B 3
2	Le Claire	g11
8	Le Mars	B 1
2	Leon	D 4
1	Lisbon	C 6
2	Logan	C 2
2	Madrid	C 4, e 8
5	Manchester	B 6
1	Manly	A 4
2	Manning	C 2
2	Manson	B 3
2	Mapleton	B 2
6	Maquoketa	B 7
1	Marcus	B 2
2	Marengo	C 5
15	Marion	B 6
23	Marshalltown	B 5
31	Mason City	A 4
1	Mechanicsville	C 6
1	Milford	A 2
4	Missouri Valley	C 2
3	Monticello	B 6
2	Mount Ayr	D 3
7	Mount Pleasant	D 6
3	Mount Vernon	C 6
22	Muscatine	C 6
2	Nashua	B 5
2	Nevada	B 4
4	New Hampton	A 5
2	New London	D 6
15	Newton	C 4
2	Northwood	A 4
3	Norwoodville	e 8
8	Oelwein	B 6
2	Ogden	B 3
3	Onawa	B 1
3	Orange City	A 1
4	Osage	B 5
2	Osceola	C 4
12	Oskaloosa	C 5
34	Ottumwa	C 5
6	Pella	C 5
6	Perry	C 3
2	Pocahontas	B 3
2	Postville	A 6
6	Red Oak	D 2
2	Reinbeck	B 5
3	Rock Rapids	A 1
2	Rock Valley	A 1
2	Rockwell City	B 3
3	Sac City	B 2
4	Sheldon	A 2
3	Shenandoah	D 2
3	Sibley	A 2
2	Sigourney	C 5
2	Sioux Center	A 1
89	Sioux City	B 1
10	Spencer	A 2
3	Spirit Lake	A 2
8	Storm Lake	B 2
2	Sumner	B 5
2	Tama	C 5
3	Tipton	C 6
3	Toledo	C 5
2	Traer	B 5
10	Urbandale	C 4, e 8
2	Villisca	D 3
5	Vinton	B 5
2	Wapello	C 6
6	Washington	C 6
74	Waterloo	B 5
4	Waukon	A 6
7	Waverly	B 5
9	Webster City	B 4
3	West Burlington	D 6
14	West Des Moines	C 4, e 8
3	West Union	B 6
2	Wilton Junction	C 6
6	Windsor Heights	e 8
4	Winterset	C 4

°Not shown on map. Index key denotes approximate location.

KANSAS

KANSAS
Principal Cities
Pop.—Thousands

Pop	City	Grid
7	Abilene	D 6
3	Anthony	E 5
14	Arkansas City	E 6
13	Atchison	C 8
2	Atwood	C 2
6	Augusta	E 7, g13
2	Baldwin City	D 8
4	Baxter Springs	E 9
2	Belle Plaine	E 6
4	Beloit	C 5
1	Blue Rapids	C 7
3	Bonner Springs	C 9, k16
2	Burlington	D 8
2	Caldwell	E 6
3	Caney	E 8
11	Chanute	E 8
1	Chapman	D 6
3	Cherryvale	E 8
2	Chetopa	E 8
1	Cimarron	E 3
5	Clay Center	C 6
1	Clearwater	E 6, h11
17	Coffeyville	E 8
1	Coldwater	E 4
3	Columbus	E 9
7	Concordia	C 6
1	Conway Springs	E 6
1	Cottonwood Falls	D 7
3	Council Grove	D 7
6	Derby	E 6, g12
1	De Soto	D 9, m16
2	Dighton	D 3
14	Dodge City	E 3
1	Douglass	E 7, h12
1	Downs	C 5
1	Eastborough	g12
13	El Dorado	E 7, g13
2	Elkhart	E 2
3	Ellinwood	D 5
2	Ellis	D 4
2	Ellsworth	D 5
1	Elwood	C 9
18	Emporia	D 7
1	Enterprise	D 6
1	Erie	E 8
2	Eudora	D 8, m15
4	Eureka	E 7
2	Fairdale	C 9, k16
5	Fairway	k16
9	Fort Scott	E 9
1	Frankfort	C 7
3	Fredonia	E 8
2	Frontenac	E 9
4	Galena	E 9
12	Garden City	E 3
2	Gardner	D 9
3	Garnett	D 8
2	Girard	E 9
4	Goodland	C 2
17	Great Bend	D 5
2	Greensburg	E 4
2	Halstead	E 6, g11
2	Harper	E 5
12	Hays	D 4
6	Haysville	g12
4	Herington	D 7
3	Hiawatha	C 8
2	Hill City	C 4
2	Hillsboro	D 6
4	Hoisington	D 5
3	Holton	C 8
2	Horton	C 8
1	Howard	E 7
1	Hoxie	C 3
3	Hugoton	E 2
2	Humboldt	E 8
38	Hutchinson	D 6, f11
11	Independence	E 8
7	Iola	E 8
1	Jetmore	D 4
19	Junction City	C 7
122	Kansas City	C 9, k16
4	Kingman	E 5, g10
2	Kinsley	E 4
2	Kiowa	E 5
2	La Crosse	D 4

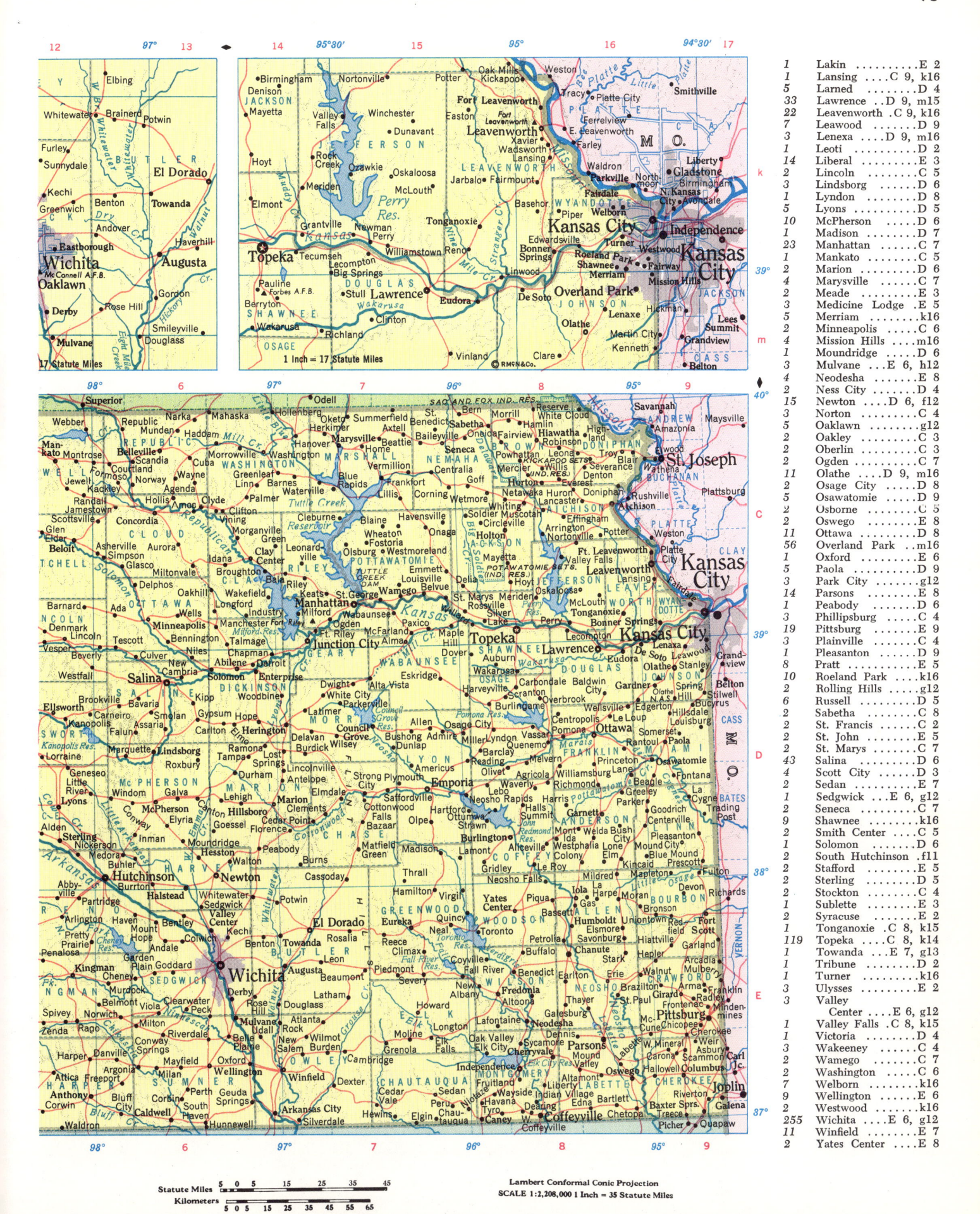

#	Name	Ref
1	Lakin	E 2
1	Lansing	C 9, k16
5	Larned	D 4
33	Lawrence	D 9, m15
22	Leavenworth	C 9, k16
7	Leawood	D 9
3	Lenexa	D 9, m16
1	Leoti	D 2
14	Liberal	E 3
1	Lincoln	C 5
3	Lindsborg	D 6
1	Lyndon	D 8
5	Lyons	D 5
10	McPherson	D 6
1	Madison	D 7
23	Manhattan	C 7
1	Mankato	C 5
3	Marion	D 6
2	Marysville	C 7
2	Meade	E 3
3	Medicine Lodge	E 5
5	Merriam	k16
2	Minneapolis	C 6
4	Mission Hills	m16
1	Moundridge	D 6
3	Mulvane	E 6, h12
2	Neodesha	E 7
2	Ness City	D 4
15	Newton	D 6, g12
5	Norton	C 4
5	Oaklawn	g12
2	Oakley	C 3
2	Oberlin	C 3
2	Ogden	C 7
11	Olathe	D 9, m16
2	Osage City	D 8
5	Osawatomie	D 9
2	Usborne	C 5
2	Oswego	E 8
11	Ottawa	D 8
56	Overland Park	m16
1	Oxford	E 6
5	Paola	D 9
3	Park City	g12
14	Parsons	E 8
1	Peabody	D 6
3	Phillipsburg	C 4
19	Pittsburg	E 9
2	Plainville	C 4
1	Pleasanton	D 9
8	Pratt	E 5
10	Roeland Park	k16
2	Rolling Hills	g12
6	Russell	D 5
2	Sabetha	C 8
2	St. Francis	C 2
2	St. John	E 5
2	St. Marys	C 7
43	Salina	D 6
2	Scott City	D 3
2	Sedan	E 7
2	Sedgwick	E 6, g12
2	Seneca	C 7
9	Shawnee	k16
5	Smith Center	C 5
1	Solomon	D 6
2	South Hutchinson	f11
2	Stafford	E 5
2	Sterling	D 5
2	Stockton	C 4
2	Sublette	E 3
2	Syracuse	E 2
2	Tonganoxie	C 8, k15
119	Topeka	C 8, k14
1	Towanda	E 7, g13
1	Tribune	D 2
1	Turner	k16
3	Ulysses	E 2
3	Valley Center	E 6, g12
1	Valley Falls	C 8, k15
1	Victoria	D 4
3	Wakeeney	C 4
2	Wamego	C 7
2	Washington	C 6
7	Welborn	k16
9	Wellington	E 6
2	Westwood	k16
255	Wichita	E 6, g12
11	Winfield	E 7
2	Yates Center	E 8

At harvest time in Kansas, ranks of combine machines line up with military precision in the wide-sweeping wheatfields.

KANSAS

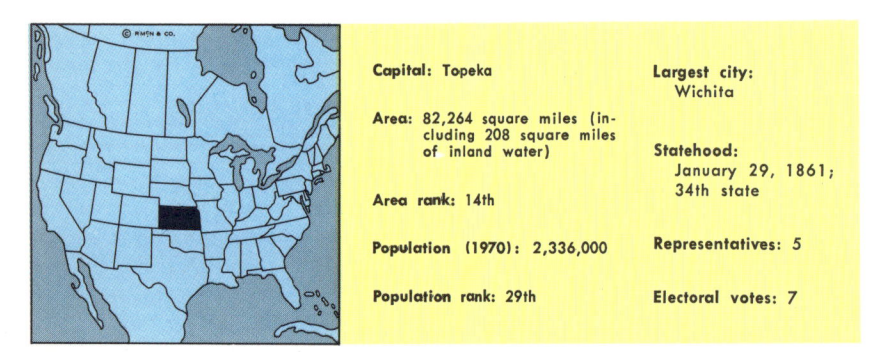

Capital: Topeka

Area: 82,264 square miles (including 208 square miles of inland water)

Area rank: 14th

Population (1970): 2,336,000

Population rank: 29th

Largest city: Wichita

Statehood: January 29, 1861; 34th state

Representatives: 5

Electoral votes: 7

Kansas is the wheat state. It produces more wheat than any other state in the Union. At harvest time (late June in Kansas), freight trains loaded entirely with wheat roll along the railways toward Kansas City or other storage and milling centers. One might think that, to produce so much, Kansas must be an endless ocean of wheat, but it is not. It is among the first five states in the number of cattle it feeds. Cattle graze on millions of acres of Kansas land, and Kansas farmers plant millions of acres of sorghum, corn, and hay crops to feed them. The heaviest wheat production is in the south central and southwestern parts of the state.

Kansas has no mountains, but it rises from an elevation of less than 750 feet along the eastern edge to more than 4,000 in places on the western border. Across the center there is a wide band of very hilly land. The hills divide the prairies on the east from the Great Plains that rise steadily to the western border.

Nearly all of Kansas had grass as its natural plant cover. Along the rivers there were narrow borders of trees, mostly cottonwoods and willows. In the east, the grass was tall and close-growing, in the west it was short and grew in clumps, or bunches.

The eastern part of the state now has varied crops, with a great deal of corn. The average rainfall is more than 30 inches. The western part of the state is drier, wheat and sorghum are the main crops, and there are miles and miles of grazing land. The west still is much like the vast empty spaces the pioneers first saw, and even now it has relatively few people, towns, roads, and railways.

During the late 1860's and the 1870's, railroads were being built westward across Kansas, and when they came Texas ranchers began driving their cattle north to the ends of the railroads for shipment east. Abilene was the first of the rough and wild "cowtowns." Later Dodge City, then called Dodge, became the main shipping point. Cattlemen turned the grasslands of Kansas into ranches, and farmers began to settle along the railways.

Kansas pioneer women are commemorated in this statue on the Capitol grounds at Topeka.

Berea College dancers perform traditional Kentucky mountain dances. Old Appalachian ways dating back to the eighteenth century are fast vanishing with extensive new highway construction in Kentucky.

KENTUCKY

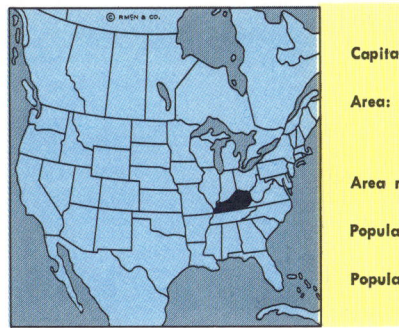

Capital: Frankfort

Area: 40,395 square miles (including 544 square miles of inland water)

Area rank: 37th

Population (1970): 3,241,000

Population rank: 23rd

Largest city: Louisville

Statehood: June 1, 1792; 15th state

Representatives: 7

Electoral votes: 9

In Kentucky two minerals, coal and limestone, have had a great influence on where people have chosen to settle and how prosperous they have become. The eastern end of the state reaches into the Appalachian Highlands, where layers of coal are buried in the rocks. Kentuckians mine more than $300,000,000 worth of high-grade coal each year, but in this part of the state, the soils are stony and the slopes steep. Farmers do poorly.

The best favored lands of Kentucky's middle elevations have stone soils—soils created by the crumbling of limestone rock. Limestone soils are fertile and productive, and such delicacies as tender bibb lettuce, also called limestone lettuce, can be grown in them. Tall, lush bluegrass and fine race horses are raised in the district around Lexington, as is almost the entire American crop of the light, aromatic, Burley tobacco.

The Highland Rim, around Bowling Green and Hopkinsville between the Cumberland and Green rivers, is another fertile limestone area where other varieties of tobacco grow, and in the Ohio River Valley, near Owensboro, dark tobacco is produced.

The state's best-known natural wonder, Mammoth Cave, is formed of limestone. It was created, over the centuries, as underground water dissolved away the rock.

Corn is one of the Blue Grass State's most valuable crops, but most of this is not marketed directly. Back in the eighteenth century, pioneer settlers realized that the most profitable and least bulky way to ship their grain east was in the form of whisky. Bourbon County, Kentucky, developed a distinctive kind of corn whisky, and distilling became a major Kentucky industry.

Kentucky was explored, beginning in 1769, by Daniel Boone, who entered from Tennessee through the Cumberland Gap. The first settlement was established in 1775. The following year Kentucky was organized as a county of Virginia. It was admitted to the Union in 1792 as the fifteenth state, with Frankfort as its capital.

Louisville (established in 1779) is the largest city, a bustling river port in the old days, today even busier as a center for both trade and industry. Churchill Downs, at the southern edge of Louisville, is the scene of a famous horserace—the Kentucky Derby.

Thoroughbred horses at pasture on a farm near Lexington in the world-famous Bluegrass Region in north-central Kentucky.

KENTUCKY

KENTUCKY
Principal Cities
Pop.—Thousands

Pop	City	Grid
2	Albany	D 4
1	Anchorage	g11
1	Artemus	D 6
31	Ashland	B 7
1	Auburn	D 3
1	Augusta	B 6
3	Barbourville	D 6
5	Bardstown	C 4
1	Bardwell	f 9
1	Beattyville	C 6
2	Beaver Dam	C 3
1	Belfry	C 7
9	Bellevue	h13
2	Benham	D 7
3	Benton	f 9
4	Berea	C 5
28	Bowling Green	D 3
2	Brandenburg	C 3
9	Buechel	B 4, g11
2	Burkesville	D 4
2	Cadiz	D 2, f10
1	Calvert City	e 9
7	Campbellsville	C 4
2	Carlisle	B 5
3	Carrollton	B 4
4	Catlettsburg	B 7
1	Cave City	C 4
4	Central City	C 2
1	Clay	C 2
2	Clinton	f 9
1	Cloverport	C 3
2	Columbia	C 4
7	Corbin	C 6
60	Covington	A 5, h13
4	Cumberland	D 7
6	Cynthiana	B 5
9	Danville	C 5
9	Dayton	h14
3	Earlington	C 2
4	East Somerset	C 5
2	Eddyville	e 9
10	Elizabethtown	C 4
1	Elkhorn City	C 7
1	Elkton	D 2
5	Elsmere	B 5, k13
2	Eminence	B 4
7	Erlanger	A 5, h13
1	Evarts	D 6
3	Fairdale	B 4, g11
3	Falmouth	B 5
6	Fern Creek	g11
4	Flatwoods	B 7
2	Flemingsburg	B 6
6	Florence	A 5, k13
15	Fort Thomas	h14
2	Fort Wright	h13
18	Frankfort	B 5
5	Franklin	D 3
1	Fullerton	B 7
3	Fulton	f 9
7	Georgetown	B 5
10	Glasgow	C 4
2	Grayson	B 7
2	Greensburg	C 4
1	Greenup	B 7
3	Greenville	C 2
1	Guthrie	D 2
1	Hardinsburg	C 3
4	Harlan	D 6
6	Harrodsburg	C 5
2	Hartford	C 3
6	Hazard	C 6
17	Henderson	C 2
2	Hickman	f 8
2	Hodgenville	C 4
19	Hopkinsville	D 2
2	Horse Cave	C 4
3	Irvine	C 6
1	Irvington	C 3
2	Jackson	C 6
5	Jeffersontown	B 4, g11
3	Jenkins	C 7
1	Junction City	C 5
1	Kenvir	D 6
2	La Grange	B 4
2	Lakeside Park	h13
3	Lancaster	C 5
3	Lawrenceburg	B 5

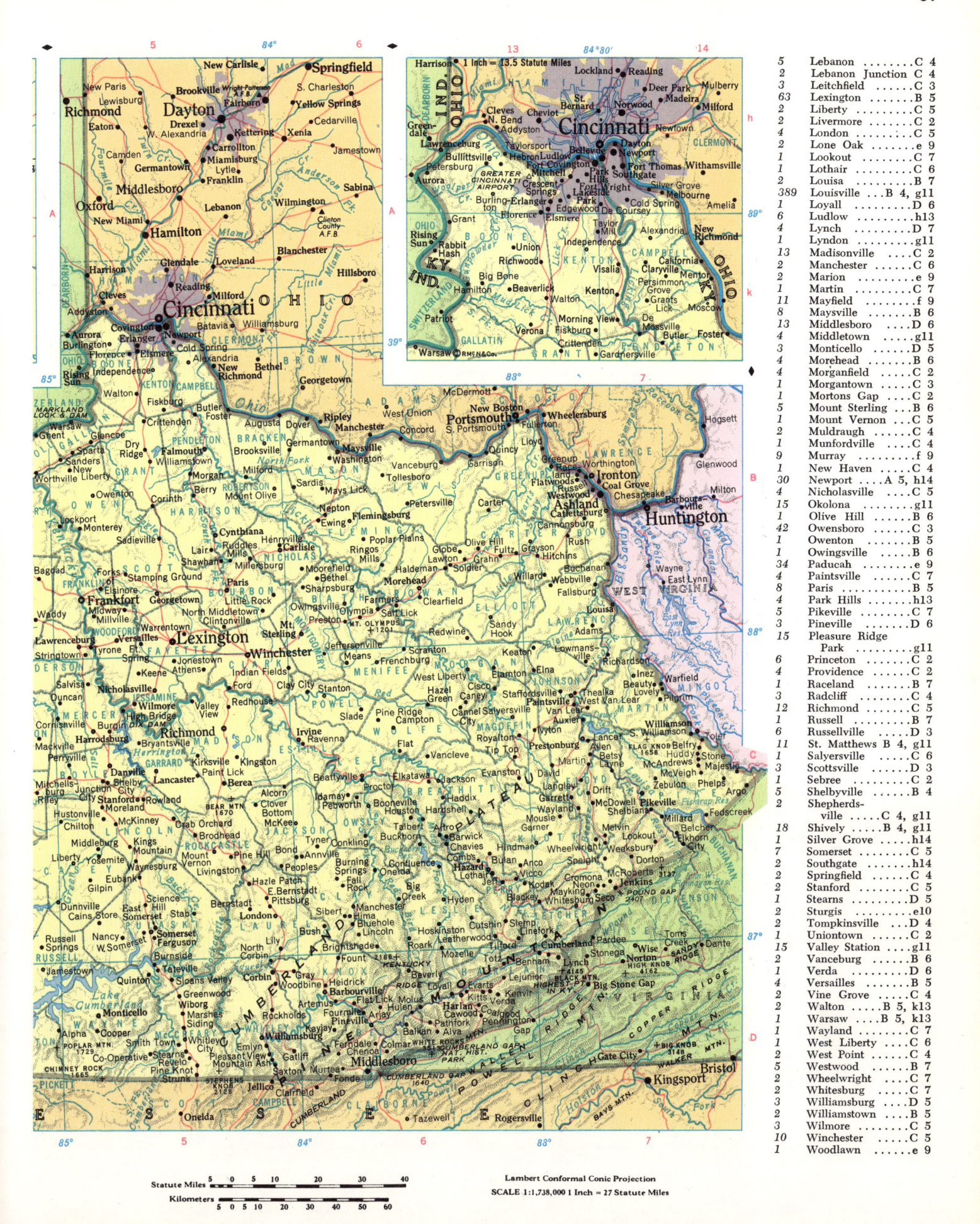

5	Lebanon	C 4
2	Lebanon Junction	C 4
3	Leitchfield	C 3
63	Lexington	B 5
2	Liberty	C 5
2	Livermore	C 2
4	London	C 5
2	Lone Oak	e 9
1	Lookout	C 7
1	Lothair	C 6
2	Louisa	B 7
389	Louisville	B 4, g11
1	Loyall	D 6
6	Ludlow	h13
4	Lynch	D 7
1	Lyndon	g11
13	Madisonville	C 2
2	Manchester	C 6
2	Marion	e 9
1	Martin	C 7
11	Mayfield	f 9
8	Maysville	B 6
13	Middlesboro	D 6
2	Middletown	g11
3	Monticello	D 5
4	Morehead	B 6
4	Morganfield	C 2
1	Morgantown	C 3
1	Mortons Gap	C 2
5	Mount Sterling	B 6
1	Mount Vernon	C 5
2	Muldraugh	C 4
1	Munfordville	C 4
9	Murray	f 9
1	New Haven	C 4
30	Newport	A 5, h14
4	Nicholasville	C 5
15	Okolona	g11
1	Olive Hill	B 6
42	Owensboro	C 3
2	Owenton	B 5
1	Owingsville	B 6
34	Paducah	e 9
4	Paintsville	C 7
4	Paris	B 5
4	Park Hills	h13
5	Pikeville	C 7
3	Pineville	D 6
15	Pleasure Ridge Park	g11
6	Princeton	C 2
4	Providence	C 2
1	Raceland	B 7
3	Radcliff	C 4
12	Richmond	C 5
1	Russell	B 7
6	Russellville	D 3
11	St. Matthews	B 4, g11
2	Salyersville	C 6
2	Scottsville	D 3
2	Sebree	C 2
5	Shelbyville	B 4
1	Shepherdsville	C 4, g11
18	Shively	B 4, g11
1	Silver Grove	h14
7	Somerset	C 5
2	Southgate	h14
2	Springfield	C 4
2	Stanford	C 5
1	Stearns	D 5
2	Sturgis	e10
1	Tompkinsville	D 4
2	Uniontown	C 2
15	Valley Station	g11
2	Vanceburg	B 6
1	Verda	D 6
4	Versailles	B 5
2	Vine Grove	C 4
2	Walton	B 5, k13
2	Warsaw	B 5, k13
1	Wayland	C 7
1	West Liberty	C 6
2	West Point	C 4
5	Westwood	B 7
2	Wheelwright	C 7
1	Whitesburg	C 7
3	Williamsburg	D 5
2	Williamstown	B 5
3	Wilmore	C 5
10	Winchester	C 5
1	Woodlawn	e 9

LOUISIANA

LOUISIANA
Principal Cities

Pop.—Thousands

Pop	City	Grid
10	Abbeville	E 3
40	Alexandria	C 3
1	Amelia	E 4, k 9
3	Amite	D 5
12	Arabi	k11
3	Arcadia	B 3
1	Arnaudville	D 4
5	Baker	D 4
2	Baldwin	E 4
1	Barataria	E 5, k11
2	Basile	D 3
15	Bastrop	B 4
152	Baton Rouge	D 4, h 9
1	Benton	B 2
2	Bernice	B 3
4	Berwick	E 4, k 9
21	Bogalusa	D 6
33	Bossier City	B 2
1	Boyce	C 3
3	Breaux Bridge	D 4
2	Broussard	D 4
5	Bunkie	D 3
4	Buras	E 6
1	Cameron	E 2
1	Campti	C 2
2	Carencro	D 3
1	Carville	h 9
16	Chalmette	E 5, k11
1	Chauvin	E 5
1	Cheneyville	C 3
4	Church Point	D 3
2	Clinton	D 4
2	Colfax	C 3
1	Columbia	B 3
2	Cottonport	C 3
1	Cotton Valley	B 2
2	Coushatta	B 2
7	Covington	D 5, h11
16	Crowley	D 3
2	Cullen	B 2
1	Cut Off	E 5
2	Delcambre	E 4
3	Delhi	B 4
4	De Quincy	D 2
7	De Ridder	D 2
6	Donaldsonville	D 4, h10
1	Doyline	B 2
1	Dubach	B 3
1	Duson	D 3
1	Elizabeth	D 3
2	Elton	D 3
2	Erath	E 3
11	Eunice	D 3
3	Farmerville	B 3
5	Ferriday	C 4
9	Franklin	E 4
3	Franklinton	D 5
2	Garyville	D 5, h10
1	Gibsland	B 2
1	Glenmora	D 3
3	Golden Meadow	E 5
3	Gonzales	D 5, h10
3	Grambling	B 3
2	Gramercy	h10
1	Grand Coteau	D 3
2	Grand Isle	E 6
22	Gretna	E 5, k11
1	Gueydan	D 3
1	Hahnville	E 5, k11
11	Hammond	D 5, g11
9	Harahan	k11
11	Harvey	E 5, k11
3	Haynesville	B 2
5	Homer	B 2
23	Houma	E 5, k10
2	Independence	D 5
2	Iowa	D 2
2	Jackson	D 4
6	Jeanerette	E 4
2	Jena	C 3
12	Jennings	D 3
4	Jonesboro	B 3
2	Jonesville	C 4
5	Kaplan	D 3
17	Kenner	E 5, k11
3	Kentwood	D 5
2	Kinder	D 3

1	Krotz Springs	D 4
50	Lafayette	D 3
4	Lake Arthur	D 2
63	Lake Charles	D 2
6	Lake Providence	B 4
4	Laplace	h11
3	Larose	E 5
1	Lecompte	C 3
5	Leesville	C 2
1	Livingston	D 5, g10
2	Lockport	E 5, k10
1	Logansport	C 2
2	Luling	k11
3	Lutcher	D 5, h10
3	Mamou	D 3
2	Mandeville	D 5, h11
6	Mansfield	B 2
2	Mansura	C 3
3	Many	C 2
2	Maplewood	D 2
1	Maringouin	D 4
4	Marksville	C 3
22	Marrero	k11
2	Melville	D 4
1	Merryville	D 2
13	Minden	B 2
52	Monroe	B 3
14	Morgan City	E 4, k 9
1	Napoleonville	E 4, k 9
14	Natchitoches	C 2
1	Newellton	B 4
29	New Iberia	D 4
628	New Orleans	E 5, h11
4	New Roads	C 4
1	New Sarpy	k11
5	Norco	D 5, h11
7	Oakdale	D 3
2	Oak Grove	B 4
2	Oberlin	D 3
1	Oil City	B 2
3	Olla	C 3
17	Opelousas	D 3
3	Patterson	E 4
9	Pineville	C 3
1	Plain Dealing	B 2
8	Plaquemine	D 4, h 9
5	Ponchatoula	D 5, h11
5	Port Allen	D 4, h 9
1	Port Barre	D 4
3	Port Sulphur	E 6
4	Raceland	E 5, k10
9	Rayne	D 3
4	Rayville	B 4
5	Reserve	h10
1	Ringgold	B 2
1	Roseland	D 5
14	Ruston	B 3
2	St. Francisville	D 4
2	St. Joseph	C 4
6	St. Martinville	D 4
1	St. Rose	k11
21	Scotlandville	D 4, g 9
1	Seymourville	h 9
161	Shreveport	B 2
2	Simmesport	D 4
6	Slidell	D 6, h12
1	Sorrento	D 5, h10
6	Springhill	A 2
1	Sterlington	B 3
11	Sulphur	D 2
3	Sunset	D 3
9	Tallulah	B 4
13	Thibodaux	E 5, k10
1	Urania	C 3
1	Vacherie	h10
4	Vidalia	C 4
8	Ville Platte	D 3
3	Vinton	D 2
3	Vivian	B 2
1	Washington	D 3
1	Waterproof	C 4
1	Weeks	E 4
3	Welsh	D 3
3	Westlake	D 2
15	West Monroe	B 3
10	Westwego	E 5, k11
2	White Castle	D 4, h 9
7	Winnfield	C 3
4	Winnsboro	B 4
3	Zachary	D 4

Ships being loaded with grain at New Orleans, one of the nation's leading seaports. The Mississippi River is in the background.

LOUISIANA

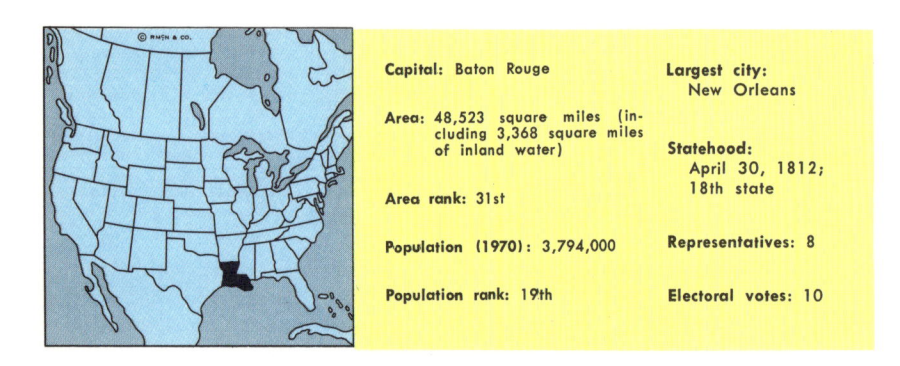

Capital: Baton Rouge

Area: 48,523 square miles (including 3,368 square miles of inland water)

Area rank: 31st

Population (1970): 3,794,000

Population rank: 19th

Largest city: New Orleans

Statehood: April 30, 1812; 18th state

Representatives: 8

Electoral votes: 10

Subtropical climate, sub-surface riches, great rivers, and a location at the mouth of the Mississippi—these factors have greatly influenced the development of Louisiana, old in history, new in technology, traditional in cherishing local customs, and international in trade.

French settlers founded the city of New Orleans in 1718. It became the key to trade with the interior, the headquarters for banking and commerce, transshipment point between riverboat and ocean vessel, a cosmopolitan French capital in the New World. Today much of its French flavor remains—particularly in the Old Quarter, where the buildings, the shops and the market, and the wonderful food in the many fine restaurants still bear the stamp of the past.

The French colony of Louisiana was ceded to Spain in 1762, ceded back in 1800, and sold to the United States in 1803. It included land, vaguely bounded, west of the Mississippi, north of Texas, east of the Rockies, and south of British Canada. It was a $15,000,000 real estate bargain. Louisiana, as it is now, was granted statehood in 1812.

It is a low-lying, hot-summer warm-winter region. The southern part of the state has only an occasional frost.

Underneath its rich soil, Louisiana has richness of a different sort. Salt, in dome-shaped underground deposits, and sulfur in other domes. Sulfur is mined by pumping hot water down a pipe and forcing the water-sulfur mixture up in a second pipe. Petroleum and natural gas are found in the southwest, northwest, and northern parts of the state and also offshore under the water of the Gulf of Mexico. Shreveport, the state's second city, is a petroleum distribution center. Lining the Mississippi from New Orleans to Baton Rouge are refineries, petrochemical plants, and industries using oil and gas as fuel.

There are 5,000 miles of navigable waterways in the state: rivers down which to float the timber harvest, water to irrigate the rice fields, marshes where muskrats are trapped, and shallow coastal areas productive of fish, shrimp, and oysters. Some of the most beautiful scenery in Louisiana is found along the coast of the Gulf of Mexico. The state is noted for its wild life, especially for its birds, and there are many wildlife refuges.

MAINE

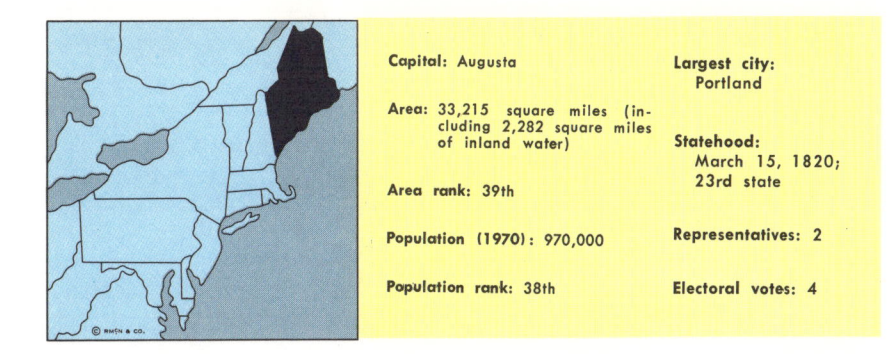

Capital: Augusta

Area: 33,215 square miles (including 2,282 square miles of inland water)

Area rank: 39th

Population (1970): 970,000

Population rank: 38th

Largest city: Portland

Statehood: March 15, 1820; 23rd state

Representatives: 2

Electoral votes: 4

Maine has the distinction of being farther east than any other state in the Union. The northern half is mountainous, except along the eastern border. Lakes of all sizes and of strange, irregular shapes occupy one-fifteenth of the state, and marshes extend the watery area much farther. Except along the eastern margin, the whole northern part of the state has no railways or improved roads, and almost no inhabitants. However, it is one of the finest areas of forest wilderness in the country, wonderful for camping, hunting, and fishing. About 80 per cent of the entire state is still covered with forests and woodland.

The irregular coast is valuable to Maine. It has long been one of the most popular resort and vacation areas on the Atlantic coast. Fishing boats of all kinds and sizes cluster in the bays and inlets. Maine lobsters are famous throughout the country, and many a lover of sea food considers lobstering Maine's most important industry. Clams, scallops, and lobsters all come from waters that are close inshore. Fishermen also go out to the banks, far from the coast, and bring back the loads of herring and perch that make up the largest part of the catch. Many coastal towns have fish canneries or packing and freezing plants.

Forests are Maine's most valuable resource. They supply the raw material for sawmills, and pulp and paper mills. Paper making is the leading industry of the state.

Maine is not a great farming state, but it has several interesting agricultural areas. Most widespread is dairy farming. Maine has a great deal of stony land that is much better for pasture than for growing crops, although farmers grow hay and oats to feed the cows during the long, snowy winters.

The largest farming region is in the northeast, in Aroostook County. This region makes Maine second only to Idaho in potato growing, and the quality of the Maine potatoes is so high that farmers all over the country buy them for planting. Blueberries are another special crop grown by Maine farmers.

Portland is the largest city of Maine and the leading port; Augusta, the capital, and Bangor both have lumber mills and paper mills, and textiles are manufactured in Lewiston and several other cities.

The waters of the Atlantic swirl at the base of Portland lighthouse on Maine's long and broken seacoast.

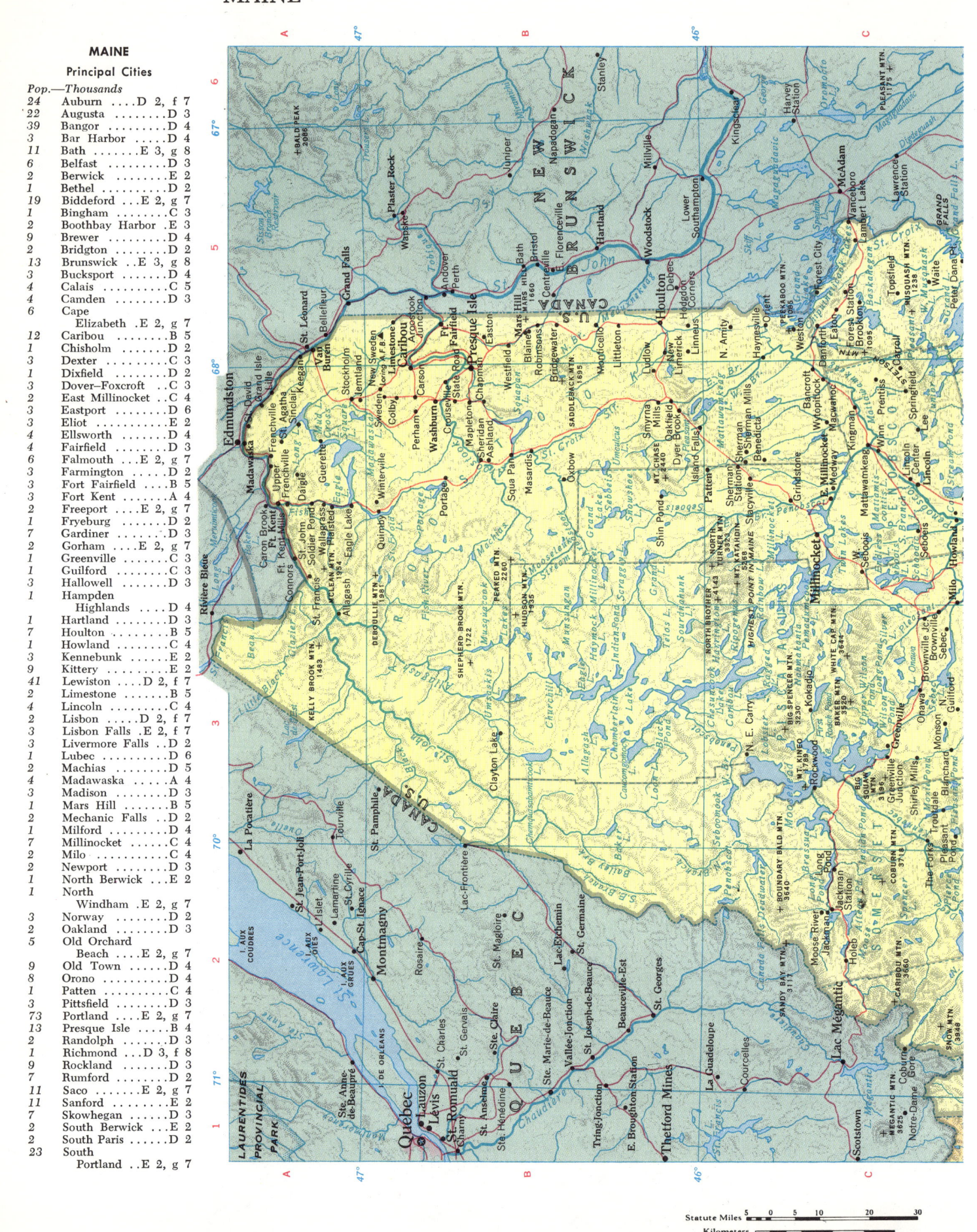

MAINE

MAINE
Principal Cities

Pop.—Thousands		
24	Auburn	D 2, f 7
22	Augusta	D 3
39	Bangor	D 4
3	Bar Harbor	D 4
11	Bath	E 3, g 8
6	Belfast	D 3
2	Berwick	E 2
1	Bethel	D 2
19	Biddeford	E 2, g 7
1	Bingham	C 3
2	Boothbay Harbor	E 3
9	Brewer	D 4
2	Bridgton	D 2
13	Brunswick	E 3, g 8
3	Bucksport	D 4
4	Calais	C 5
4	Camden	D 3
6	Cape Elizabeth	E 2, g 7
12	Caribou	B 5
1	Chisholm	D 2
3	Dexter	C 3
1	Dixfield	D 2
3	Dover–Foxcroft	C 3
2	East Millinocket	C 4
3	Eastport	D 6
3	Eliot	E 2
4	Ellsworth	D 4
4	Fairfield	D 3
6	Falmouth	E 2, g 7
3	Farmington	D 2
5	Fort Fairfield	B 5
3	Fort Kent	A 4
2	Freeport	E 2, g 7
1	Fryeburg	D 2
7	Gardiner	D 3
2	Gorham	E 2, g 7
1	Greenville	C 3
1	Guilford	C 3
3	Hallowell	D 3
1	Hampden Highlands	D 4
1	Hartland	D 3
7	Houlton	B 5
1	Howland	C 4
3	Kennebunk	E 2
9	Kittery	E 2
41	Lewiston	D 2, f 7
2	Limestone	B 5
4	Lincoln	C 4
2	Lisbon	D 2, f 7
3	Lisbon Falls	E 2, f 7
3	Livermore Falls	D 2
1	Lubec	D 6
2	Machias	D 5
1	Madawaska	A 4
3	Madison	D 3
1	Mars Hill	B 5
2	Mechanic Falls	D 2
1	Milford	D 4
7	Millinocket	C 4
2	Milo	C 4
2	Newport	D 3
2	North Berwick	E 2
1	North Windham	E 2, g 7
3	Norway	D 2
2	Oakland	D 3
5	Old Orchard Beach	E 2, g 7
9	Old Town	D 4
2	Orono	D 4
1	Patten	C 4
3	Pittsfield	D 3
73	Portland	E 2, g 7
13	Presque Isle	B 4
2	Randolph	D 3
1	Richmond	D 3, f 8
9	Rockland	D 3
7	Rumford	D 2
11	Saco	E 2, g 7
11	Sanford	E 2
7	Skowhegan	D 3
2	South Berwick	E 2
2	South Paris	D 2
23	South Portland	E 2, g 7

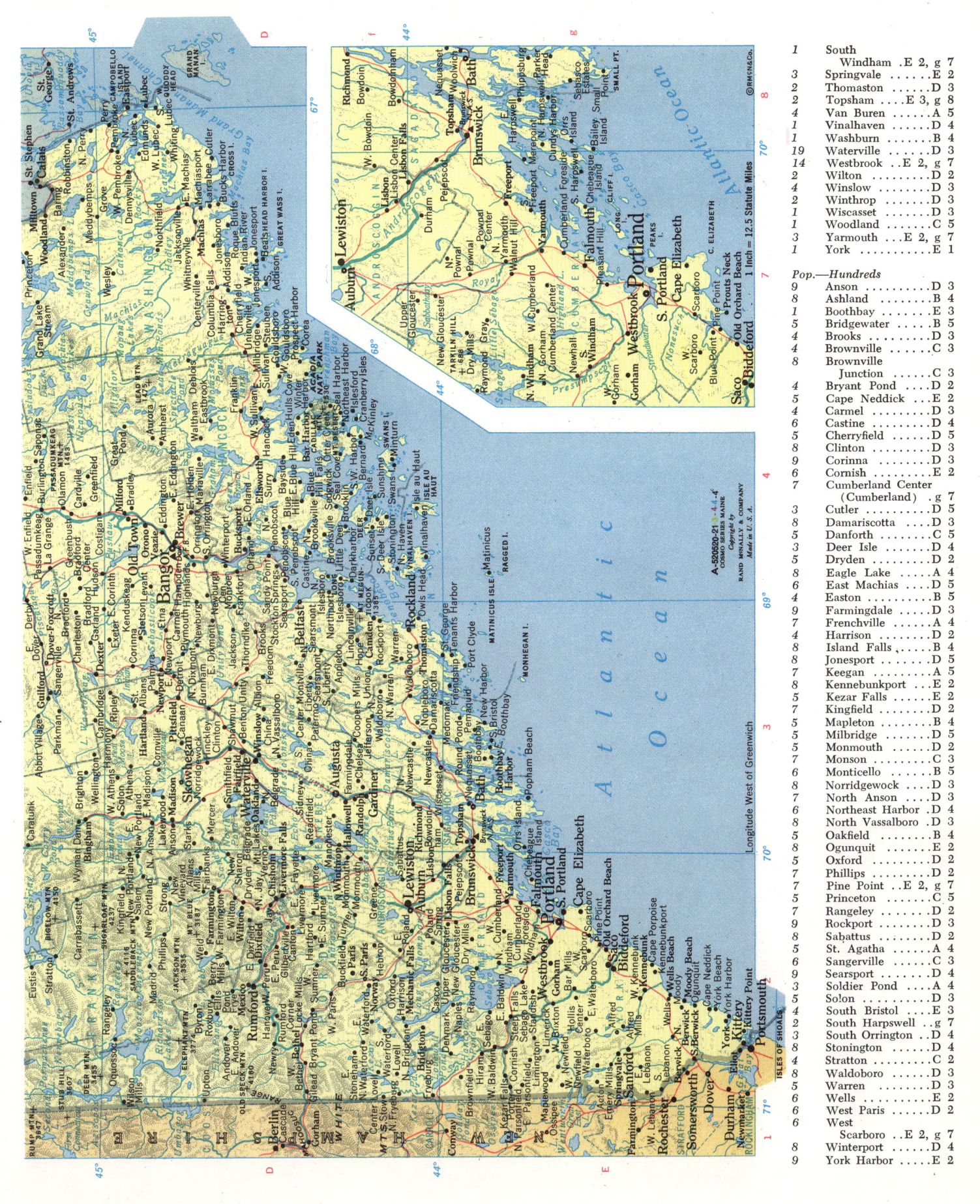

1	South Windham	E 2, g 7
3	Springvale	E 2
2	Thomaston	D 3
2	Topsham	E 3, g 8
4	Van Buren	A 5
1	Vinalhaven	D 4
1	Washburn	B 4
19	Waterville	D 3
14	Westbrook	E 2, g 7
2	Wilton	D 2
4	Winslow	D 3
2	Winthrop	D 3
1	Wiscasset	D 3
1	Woodland	C 5
3	Yarmouth	E 2, g 7
1	York	E 1

Pop.—Hundreds

9	Anson	D 3
8	Ashland	B 4
1	Boothbay	E 3
5	Bridgewater	B 5
4	Brooks	D 3
4	Brownville	C 3
8	Brownville Junction	C 3
4	Bryant Pond	D 2
5	Cape Neddick	E 2
4	Carmel	D 3
6	Castine	D 4
5	Cherryfield	D 5
4	Clinton	D 3
9	Corinna	D 3
6	Cornish	E 2
7	Cumberland Center (Cumberland)	g 7
3	Cutler	D 5
8	Damariscotta	D 3
5	Danforth	C 5
3	Deer Isle	D 4
5	Dryden	D 2
8	Eagle Lake	A 4
7	East Machias	D 5
4	Easton	B 5
4	Farmingdale	D 3
7	Frenchville	A 4
4	Harrison	D 2
8	Island Falls	B 4
8	Jonesport	D 5
6	Keegan	A 5
8	Kennebunkport	E 2
5	Kezar Falls	E 2
4	Kingfield	D 2
8	Mapleton	B 4
5	Milbridge	D 5
7	Monmouth	D 2
7	Monson	C 3
6	Monticello	B 5
8	Norridgewock	D 3
8	North Anson	D 3
6	Northeast Harbor	D 4
8	North Vassalboro	D 3
5	Oakfield	B 4
8	Ogunquit	E 2
5	Oxford	D 2
7	Phillips	D 2
7	Pine Point	E 2, g 7
7	Princeton	C 5
7	Rangeley	D 2
9	Rockport	D 3
8	Sabattus	D 2
7	St. Agatha	A 4
5	Sangerville	C 3
9	Searsport	D 4
3	Soldier Pond	A 4
7	Solon	D 3
3	South Bristol	E 3
2	South Harpswell	g 7
6	South Orrington	D 4
4	Stonington	D 4
3	Stratton	C 2
8	Waldoboro	D 3
4	Warren	D 3
4	Wells	E 2
6	West Paris	D 2
6	West Scarboro	E 2, g 7
8	Winterport	D 4
9	York Harbor	E 2

MARYLAND

MARYLAND
Principal Cities

Pop.—Thousands		
10	Aberdeen	A 5
23	Annapolis	C 5
1	Ardmore	C 4
939	Baltimore	B 4, g11
5	Baltimore Highlands	h11
4	Bel Air	A 5
7	Beltsville	B 4
2	Berlin	D 7
76	Bethesda	C 3, f 8
3	Bladensburg	f 9
1	Boonsboro	A 2
2	Boulevard Heights	f 9
1	Bowie	B 4
4	Brentwood	f 9
4	Brunswick	B 2
3	Cabin John	C 3, f 8
12	Cambridge	C 5
3	Capitol Heights	C 4, f 9
3	Carrollton	A 4
45	Catonsville	B 4, g10
2	Centreville	B 5
1	Chesapeake City	A 6
4	Chestertown	B 5
14	Chillum	f 9
4	Clinton	C 4
4	Cockeysville	B 4
18	College Park	C 4, f 9
2	Colmar Manor	f 9
2	Cresaptown	k13
4	Crisfield	E 6
33	Cumberland	k13
1	Damascus	B 3
2	Denton	C 6
8	District Heights	C 4
85	Dundalk	B 4, g11
6	Easton	C 5
1	Eckhart Mines	k13
5	Edgewood	B 5
2	Elkridge	B 4, h10
6	Elkton	A 6
2	Ellicott City	B 4
38	Essex	B 5
2	Fairmont Heights	f 9
2	Federalsburg	C 6
3	Ferndale	B 4
22	Frederick	B 3
7	Frostburg	k13
1	Fruitland	D 6
1	Funkstown	A 2
4	Gaithersburg	B 3
23	Glen Burnie	B 4
7	Greenbelt	B 4
1	Greensboro	C 6
37	Hagerstown	A 2
23	Halethorpe	B 4, h10
5	Halfway	A 2
2	Hancock	A 1
9	Havre de Grace	A 5
20	Hillcrest Heights	f 9
1	Hurlock	C 6
15	Hyattsville	C 4, f 9
2	Kensington	B 4
12	Langley Park	f 9
5	Lanham	B 4
9	Lansdowne	B 4, h11
1	LaPlata	C 4
9	Laurel	B 4
1	Leonardtown	D 4
8	Lexington Park	D 5
11	Linthicum Heights	B 4, h11
2	Lonaconing	k13
14	Lutherville-Timonium	B 4
1	Manchester	A 4
2	Marley	B 4
15	Middle River	B 5
1	Middletown	B 2
1	Mountain Lake Park	m12
10	Mount Rainier	f 9
2	Mount Savage	k13
2	North East	A 6
2	Oakland	m12
1	Ocean City	D 7
3	Odenton	B 4
12	Overlea	B 4, g11

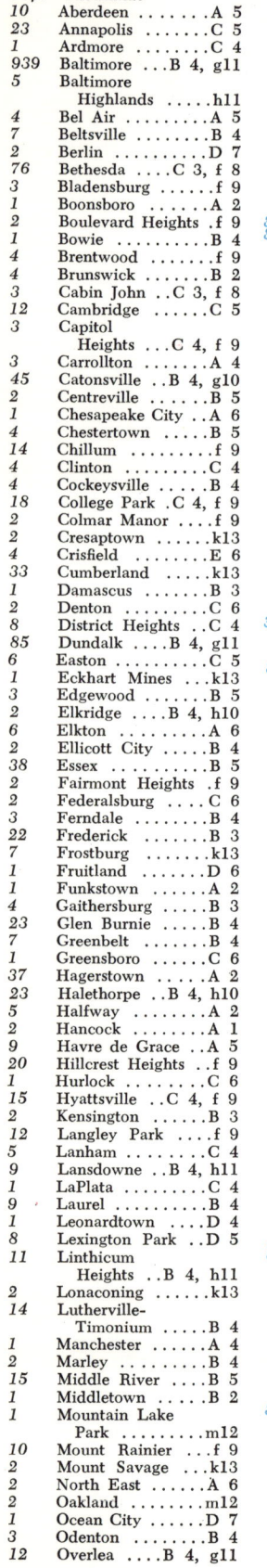

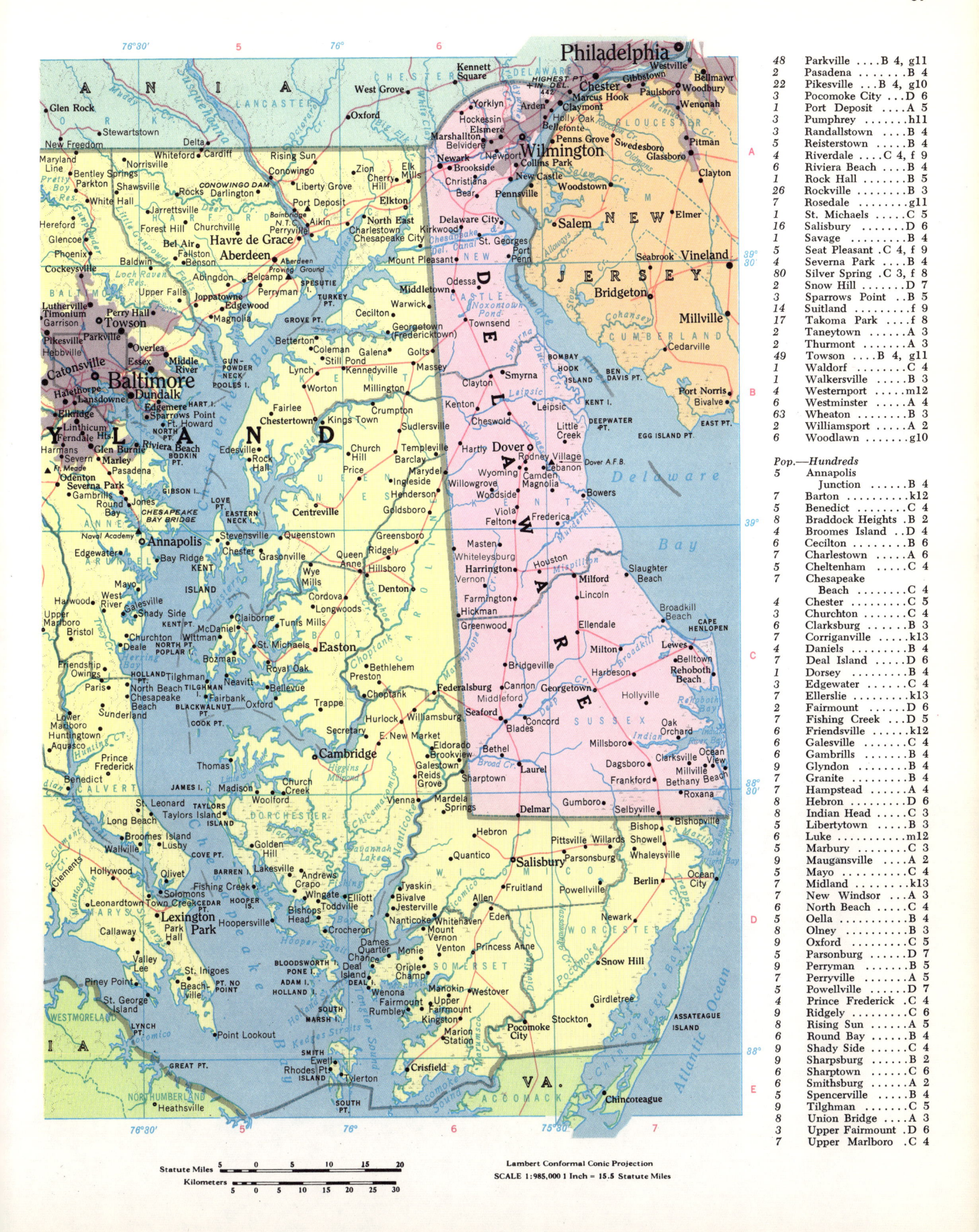

48	Parkville	B 4, g11
2	Pasadena	B 4
22	Pikesville	B 4, g10
3	Pocomoke City	D 6
1	Port Deposit	A 5
3	Pumphrey	h11
3	Randallstown	B 4
5	Reisterstown	B 4
4	Riverdale	C 4, f 9
6	Riviera Beach	B 4
1	Rock Hall	B 5
26	Rockville	B 3
7	Rosedale	g11
1	St. Michaels	C 5
16	Salisbury	D 6
1	Savage	B 4
5	Seat Pleasant	C 4, f 9
4	Severna Park	B 4
80	Silver Spring	C 3, f 8
2	Snow Hill	D 7
3	Sparrows Point	B 5
14	Suitland	f 9
17	Takoma Park	f 8
2	Taneytown	A 3
2	Thurmont	A 3
49	Towson	B 4, g11
1	Waldorf	C 4
1	Walkersville	B 3
4	Westernport	m12
6	Westminster	A 4
63	Wheaton	B 3
2	Williamsport	A 2
6	Woodlawn	g10

Pop.—Hundreds

5	Annapolis Junction	B 4
7	Barton	k12
5	Benedict	C 4
8	Braddock Heights	B 2
4	Broomes Island	D 4
6	Cecilton	B 6
7	Charlestown	A 6
5	Cheltenham	C 4
7	Chesapeake Beach	C 4
4	Chester	C 5
3	Churchton	C 4
6	Clarksburg	B 3
7	Corriganville	k13
4	Daniels	B 4
7	Deal Island	D 6
1	Dorsey	B 4
3	Edgewater	C 4
7	Ellerslie	k13
2	Fairmount	D 6
7	Fishing Creek	D 5
6	Friendsville	k12
6	Galesville	C 4
6	Gambrills	B 4
7	Glyndon	B 4
2	Granite	B 4
7	Hampstead	A 4
8	Hebron	D 6
8	Indian Head	C 3
5	Libertytown	B 3
6	Luke	m12
5	Marbury	C 3
5	Maugansville	A 2
5	Mayo	C 4
7	Midland	k13
7	New Windsor	A 3
6	North Beach	C 4
5	Oella	B 4
8	Olney	B 3
9	Oxford	C 5
7	Parsonburg	D 7
9	Perryman	B 5
7	Perryville	A 5
5	Powellville	D 7
4	Prince Frederick	C 4
9	Ridgely	C 6
8	Rising Sun	A 5
9	Round Bay	B 4
9	Shady Side	C 4
6	Sharpsburg	B 2
6	Sharptown	C 6
9	Smithsburg	A 2
5	Spencerville	B 3
9	Tilghman	C 5
8	Union Bridge	A 3
3	Upper Fairmount	D 6
7	Upper Marlboro	C 4

MARYLAND

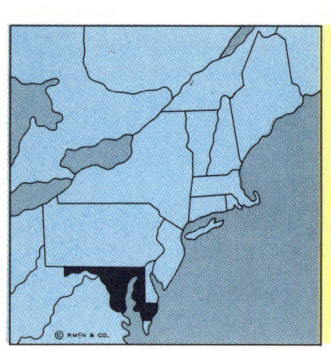

Capital: Annapolis

Area: 10,577 square miles (including 686 square miles of inland water)

Area rank: 42nd

Population (1970): 3,844,000

Population rank: 18th

Largest city: Baltimore

Statehood: April 28, 1788; 7th state

Representatives: 8

Electoral votes: 10

Maryland includes five distinct sections, each with a way of life based on its special resources. The Eastern Shore (the land east of Chesapeake Bay) enjoys mild winters and warm, humid summers. The growing season is almost seven months long, lasting from April to October. Farmers do truck gardening, growing early spring vegetables and strawberries for city markets and tomatoes for canning, or raise chickens to be marketed as broilers. The most important industry in the towns is packing, processing, and shipping the farm products.

The shores of Chesapeake Bay and its inlets, and the isolated islands in mid-bay, are the homes of many fishermen, who seem to outsiders to inhabit a world of their own. They operate fishing boats, boats that dredge up oysters and clams, or catch crabs. Other workers prepare and pack the catch, tend the crab pens and terrapin enclosures in Crisfield, the key shipping center. West of Chesapeake Bay is a strip of beautiful rolling country, good farmland wherever it is not occupied by cities. The farmers grow tobacco and feed crops for their livestock—corn, soybeans, and hay. Their dairy cows provide milk for Baltimore and Washington.

Less than 50 miles inland from Baltimore, the Appalachian highlands begin with a series of rugged ridges and deep valleys. Its inhabitants farm the valleys, work in coal mines, or in the forests, or work on the many railways that are needed to serve the industries of the area.

Still another variety of Marylander is the city-dweller. Baltimore, with its suburbs, is one of the great metropolitan districts of the United States. Maryland's settlers landed on an island in Chesapeake Bay in 1634. The capital, Annapolis, was founded in 1649; but Baltimore, established in 1729, soon outgrew the older settlements because of its superior location. Today it is one of the country's leading seaports and industrial centers.

The District of Columbia, coextensive with the city of Washington, lies along the bank of the Potomac River, a 69-square-mile tract that was formerly part of Maryland. The city was laid out by the French-born engineer Pierre L'Enfant, and was first occupied by the federal government in 1800. Maryland suburbs with over 900,000 inhabitants adjoin the Washington, D.C. area.

Civil War cannon overlook a peaceful farm on the battlefield of Antietam near Sharpsburg, Maryland.

MASSACHUSETTS

Everyone who has gone to school in the United States knows at least a little about the early days of Massachusetts. The names of Plymouth, Boston, Cape Cod, Salem, Lexington, Concord, are household words.

Massachusetts is not, on the whole, good farming country. Today most of its leading farm products are specialties. There are many dairy cows, and the dairy farmers raise hay for feed. The Connecticut Valley produces general crops, including many potatoes, but its successful tobacco farms are more famous. One of the best-known specialties of Massachusetts is its cranberry crop, grown at the landward end of Cape Cod.

From earliest colonial days, Massachusetts men were fishermen. Fish, lobsters, and clams certainly saved some of the settlers from starvation. Fishing is still a big industry, with Boston and Gloucester as its principal centers. Until the middle of the nineteenth century, New Bedford and Nantucket Island sent whaling vessels on voyages to the Pacific Ocean.

Early Massachusetts was well forested, and every port had a shipyard where fishing boats were built, and also wooden trading vessels, which were sailed by Massachusetts men to the ports of the West Indies, Europe, Asia, and Africa, and to domestic ports farther south on the Atlantic coast. The traders brought back raw materials that gave Massachusetts an early start in manufacturing.

Cotton from the South was the basis of the textile industry, in which Massachusetts was a leader until the twentieth century. Then the South became the center of cotton manufacture, but Massachusetts still has many textile mills, as well as a wide variety of other manufacturing industries.

Now Massachusetts is largely industrial and urban as far west as the Connecticut Valley. Except for a few areas such as Cape Cod, cities and towns are only a few miles apart. Highways and railroads form a close network. West of the Connecticut Valley, the population is sparser.

Massachusetts has many famous universities and colleges. Even with its crowded population, it has beautiful scenery and charming little towns.

Capital: Boston

Area: 8,257 square miles (including 424 square miles of inland water)

Area rank: 45th

Population (1970): 5,561,000

Population rank: 10th

Largest city: Boston

Statehood: February 6, 1788; 6th state

Representatives: 12

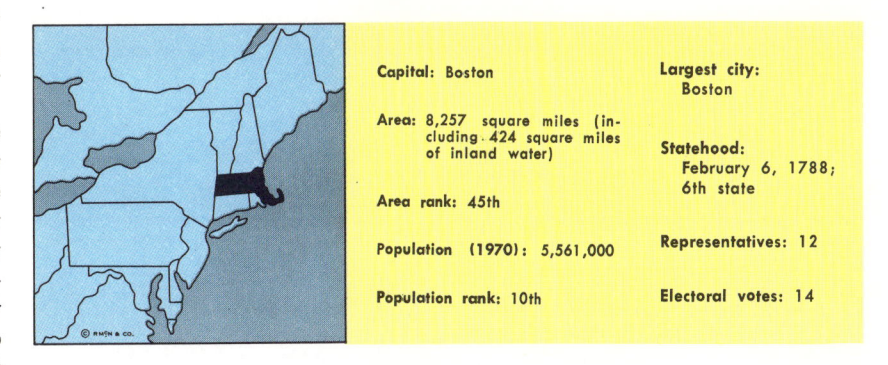

Electoral votes: 14

The "sacred codfish," symbol of the fishing industry of Massachusetts, hangs above the Chamber of the House of Representatives in the state capitol building at Boston.

MASSACHUSETTS

MASSACHUSETTS
Principal Cities

Pop.—Thousands

Pop.	City	Grid
5	Abington	B 6, h12
3	Acushnet	C 6
12	Adams	A 1
7	Agawam	B 2
11	Amesbury	A 6
15	Amherst	B 2
11	Andover	A 5
50	Arlington	B 5, g11
8	Ashland	g10
12	Athol	A 3
27	Attleboro	C 5
14	Auburn	B 4
4	Avon	B 5, h11
15	Ayer	A 4, f 9
11	Bedford	B 5, g10
29	Belmont	g11
36	Beverly	A 6, f12
697	Boston	B 5, g11
31	Braintree	B 5, h11
5	Bridgewater	C 6
73	Brockton	B 5, h11
54	Brookline	B 5, g11
3	Brookville	h11
13	Burlington	f11
108	Cambridge	B 5, g11
13	Canton	B 5, h11
4	Chelmsford	A 5, f10
34	Chelsea	B 5, g11
62	Chicopee	B 2
13	Clinton	B 4
5	Cochituate	g10
3	Cohasset	B 6, h12
5	Concord	B 5, g10
6	Dalton	B 1
22	Danvers	A 6, f12
24	Dedham	B 5, h11
12	Dracut	A 5
3	East Bridgewater	B 6
12	Easthampton	B 2
10	East Longmeadow	B 2
44	Everett	g11
14	Fairhaven	C 6
100	Fall River	C 5
3	Falmouth	C 6
5	Feeding Hills	B 2
43	Fitchburg	A 4
6	Foxboro	B 5
45	Framingham	B 5, g10
8	Franklin	B 5
19	Gardner	A 4
26	Gloucester	A 6, f13
4	Great Barrington	B 1
18	Greenfield	A 2
46	Haverhill	A 5
13	Hingham	B 6, h12
8	Holbrook	B 5, h11
3	Holliston	h11
53	Holyoke	B 2
4	Hopedale	B 4, h 9
3	Hopkinton	B 4, h 9
10	Hudson	B 4, g 9
7	Hull	B 6, g12
6	Hyannis	C 7
5	Ipswich	A 6
4	Islington	h11
71	Lawrence	A 5
3	Lee	B 1
28	Leominster	A 4
28	Lexington	B 5, g11
2	Littleton Common	f10
11	Longmeadow	B 2
92	Lowell	A 5, f10
12	Ludlow	B 3
94	Lynn	B 6, g11
8	Lynnfield	f11
58	Malden	B 5, g11
4	Manchester	A 6, f12
19	Marblehead	B 6, f12
19	Marlboro	B 4, g 9
8	Maynard	B 5, g10
65	Medford	B 5, g11
30	Melrose	B 5, g11
28	Methuen	A 5
6	Middleboro	C 6
16	Milford	B 4, h 9
6	Millbury	B 4

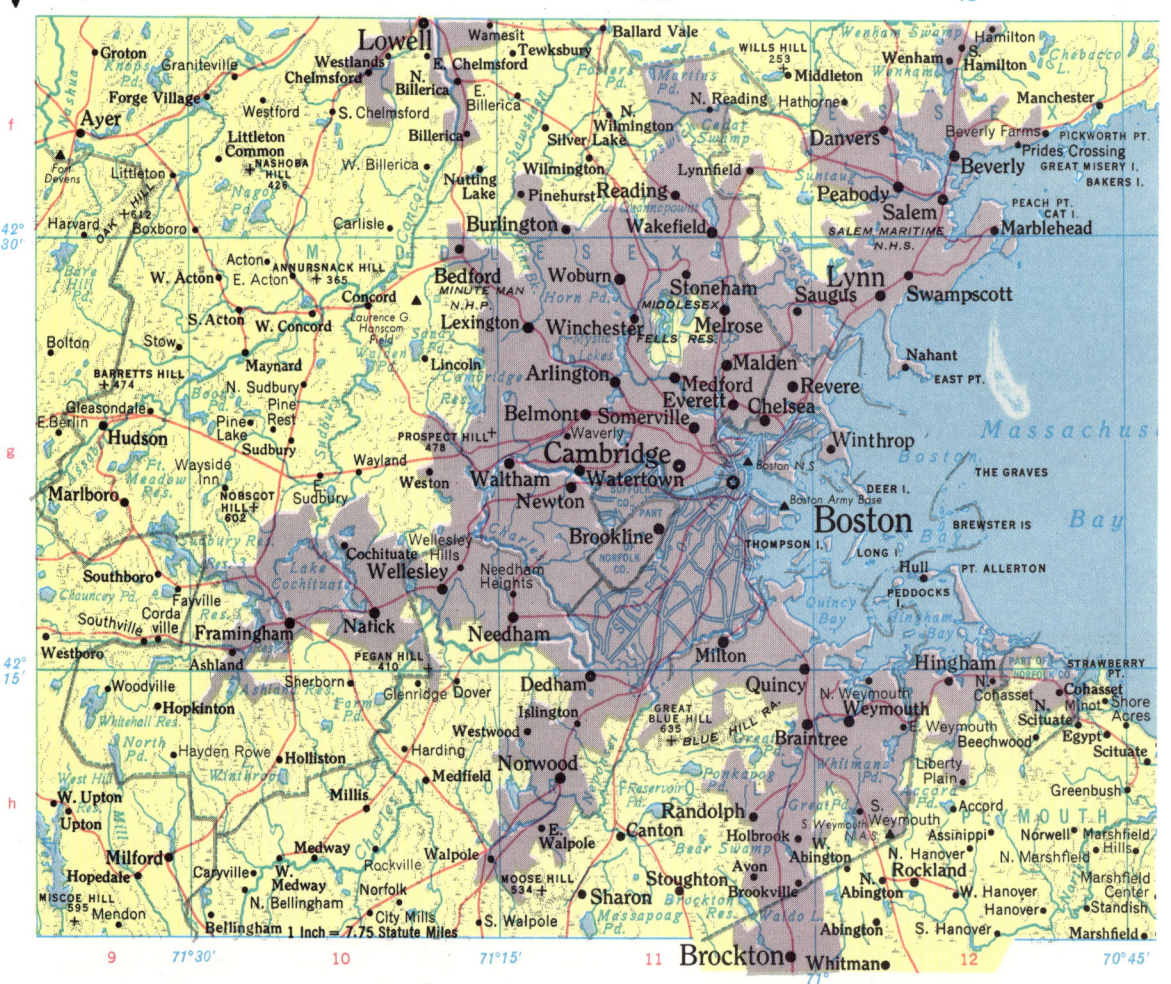

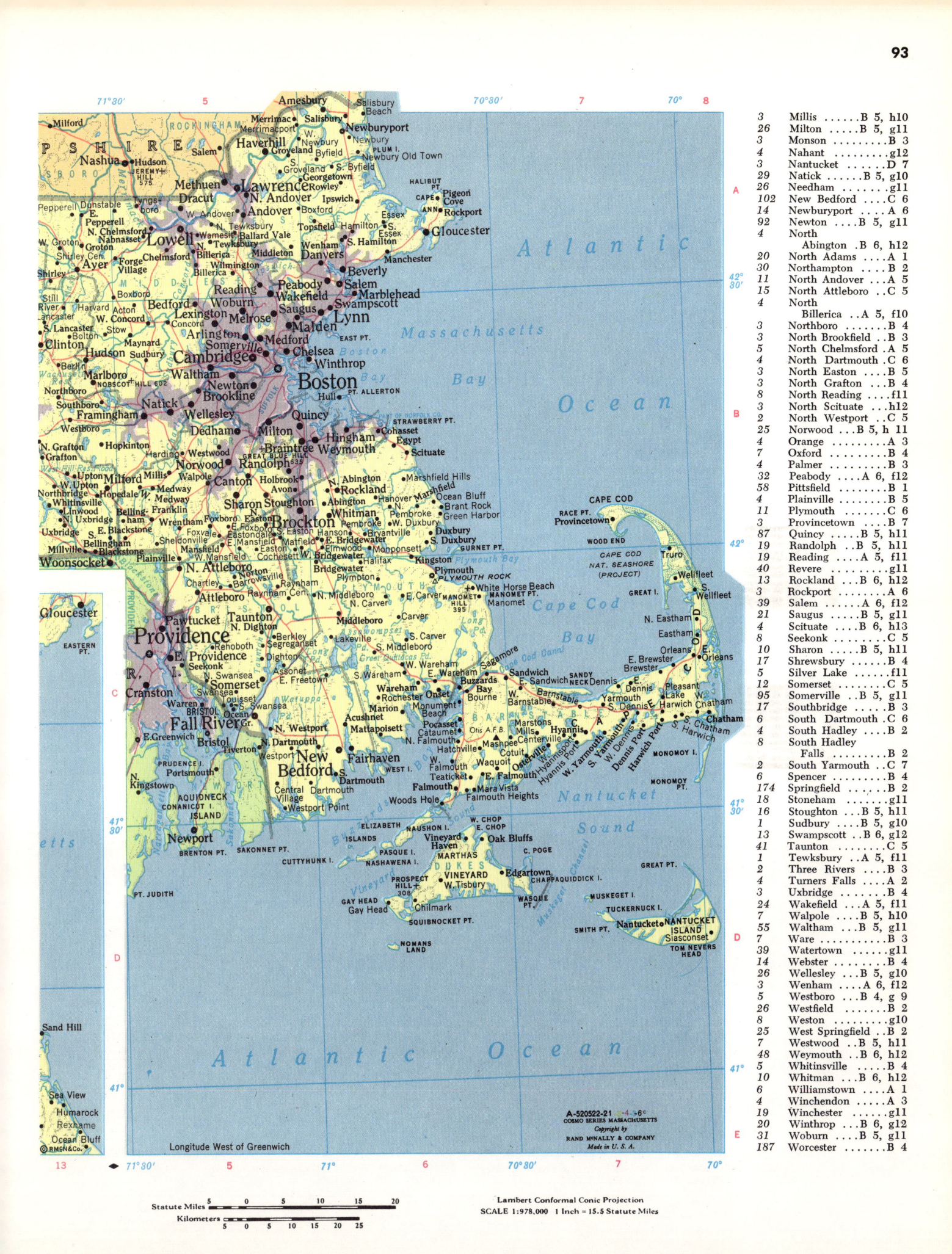

3	Millis	B 5, h10
26	Milton	B 5, g11
3	Monson	B 3
4	Nahant	g12
3	Nantucket	D 7
29	Natick	B 5, g10
26	Needham	g11
102	New Bedford	C 6
14	Newburyport	A 6
92	Newton	B 5, g11
4	North Abington	B 6, h10
20	North Adams	A 1
30	Northampton	B 2
11	North Andover	A 5
15	North Attleboro	C 5
4	North Billerica	A 5, f10
3	Northboro	B 4
3	North Brookfield	B 3
5	North Chelmsford	A 5
4	North Dartmouth	C 6
3	North Easton	B 5
3	North Grafton	B 4
17	North Reading	f11
3	North Scituate	h12
4	North Westport	C 5
25	Norwood	B 5, h 11
4	Orange	A 3
7	Oxford	B 4
4	Palmer	B 3
32	Peabody	A 6, f12
58	Pittsfield	B 1
4	Plainville	B 5
11	Plymouth	C 6
3	Provincetown	B 7
87	Quincy	B 5, h11
19	Randolph	B 5, h11
19	Reading	A 5, f11
40	Revere	g11
13	Rockland	B 6, h12
3	Rockport	A 6
39	Salem	A 6, f12
21	Saugus	B 5, g11
4	Scituate	B 6, h13
8	Seekonk	C 5
10	Sharon	B 5, h11
17	Shrewsbury	B 4
5	Silver Lake	f11
12	Somerset	C 5
95	Somerville	B 5, g11
17	Southbridge	B 3
6	South Dartmouth	C 6
4	South Hadley	B 2
8	South Hadley Falls	B 2
2	South Yarmouth	C 7
6	Spencer	B 4
174	Springfield	B 2
18	Stoneham	g11
16	Stoughton	B 5, h11
1	Sudbury	B 5, g10
13	Swampscott	B 6, g12
41	Taunton	C 5
1	Tewksbury	A 5, f11
2	Three Rivers	B 3
4	Turners Falls	A 2
3	Uxbridge	B 4
24	Wakefield	A 5, f11
7	Walpole	B 5, h10
55	Waltham	B 5, g11
3	Ware	B 3
39	Watertown	g11
14	Webster	B 4
26	Wellesley	B 5, g10
3	Wenham	A 6, f12
5	Westboro	B 4, g 9
26	Westfield	B 2
8	Weston	g10
25	West Springfield	B 2
7	Westwood	B 5, h11
48	Weymouth	B 6, h12
5	Whitinsville	B 4
10	Whitman	B 6, h12
6	Williamstown	A 1
4	Winchendon	A 3
19	Winchester	g11
20	Winthrop	B 6, g12
31	Woburn	B 5, g11
187	Worcester	B 4

MICHIGAN

MICHIGAN
Principal Cities

Pop.—Thousands

Pop	City	Grid
20	Adrian	G 6
13	Albion	F 6
3	Algonac	F 8
5	Allegan	F 5
37	Allen Park	p15
9	Alma	E 6
15	Alpena	C 7
67	Ann Arbor	F 7, p14
5	Auburn Heights	F 7
3	Bad Axe	E 8
44	Battle Creek	F 5
54	Bay City	E 7
5	Belding	E 5
19	Benton Harbor	F 4
23	Berkley	F 7, o15
3	Bessemer	n11
9	Big Rapids	E 5
26	Birmingham	F 7, o15
3	Blissfield	G 7
2	Bloomfield Hills	o15
3	Boyne City	C 6
5	Buchanan	G 4
10	Cadillac	D 5
4	Caro	E 7
7	Carrollton	E 7
3	Charlevoix	C 5
8	Charlotte	F 6
6	Cheboygan	C 6
3	Chelsea	F 6
3	Chesaning	E 6
15	Clawson	o15
9	Coldwater	G 5
5	Comstock	F 5
3	Corunna	F 6
2	Croswell	E 8
2	Crystal Falls	B 2
4	Davison	E 7
112	Dearborn	F 7, p15
2	Decatur	F 5
1,670	Detroit	F 7, p15
7	Dowagiac	G 4
14	Drayton Plains	F 7
3	Durand	F 6
46	East Detroit	p16
30	East Lansing	F 6
4	Eaton Rapids	F 6
17	Ecorse	p15
15	Escanaba	C 3
5	Essexville	E 7
9	Fair Plain	F 4
7	Farmington	p15
8	Fenton	F 7
5	Flat Rock	F 7
197	Flint	E 7
6	Flushing	E 7
2	Frankenmuth	E 7
3	Fremont	E 5
38	Garden City	p15
3	Gaylord	C 6
5	Gladstone	C 4
11	Grand Haven	E 4
5	Grand Ledge	F 6
177	Grand Rapids	F 5
8	Grandville	F 5
7	Greenville	E 5
15	Grosse Pointe Park	p16
19	Grosse Pointe Woods	p16
34	Hamtramck	p15
5	Hancock	A 2
2	Harbor Beach	E 8
26	Hazel Park	p15
38	Highland Park	p15
8	Hillsdale	G 6
25	Holland	F 4
3	Holly	F 7
5	Holt	F 6
3	Houghton	A 2
5	Howell	F 7
3	Hudson	G 6
3	Hudsonville	F 5
9	Huntington Woods	p15
39	Inkster	p15
7	Ionia	F 5
9	Iron Mountain	C 2
4	Iron River	B 2
10	Ironwood	n11
9	Ishpeming	B 3

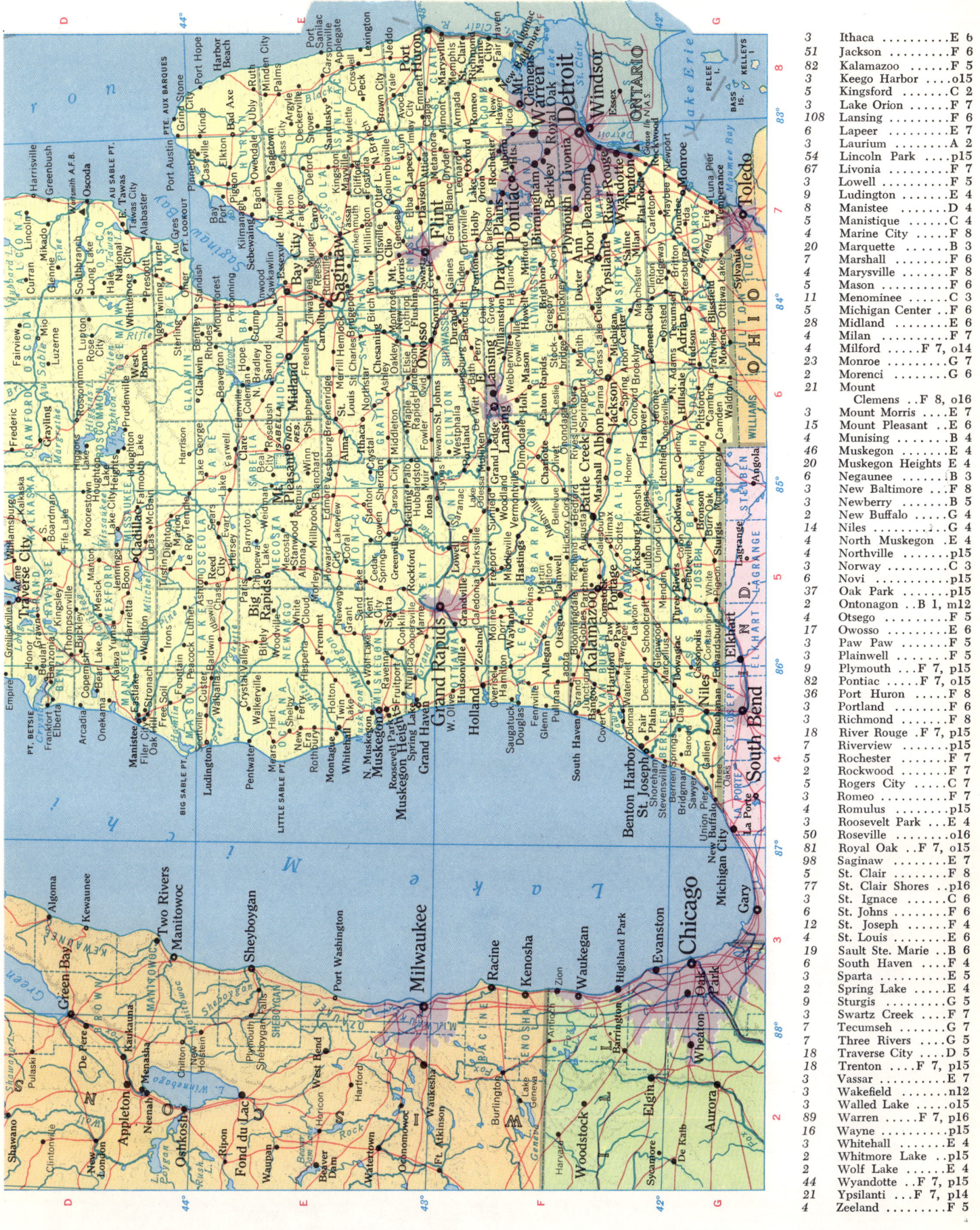

3	Ithaca	E 6
51	Jackson	F 6
82	Kalamazoo	F 5
3	Keego Harbor	o15
5	Kingsford	C 2
3	Lake Orion	F 7
108	Lansing	F 6
6	Lapeer	E 7
3	Laurium	A 2
54	Lincoln Park	p15
67	Livonia	F 7
3	Lowell	F 5
9	Ludington	E 4
8	Manistee	D 4
5	Manistique	C 4
4	Marine City	F 8
20	Marquette	B 3
7	Marshall	F 6
4	Marysville	F 8
5	Mason	F 6
11	Menominee	C 3
5	Michigan Center	F 6
28	Midland	E 6
4	Milan	F 7
4	Milford	F 7, o14
23	Monroe	G 7
2	Morenci	G 6
21	Mount Clemens	F 8, o16
3	Mount Morris	E 7
15	Mount Pleasant	E 6
4	Munising	B 4
46	Muskegon	E 4
20	Muskegon Heights	E 4
6	Negaunee	B 3
3	New Baltimore	F 8
3	Newberry	B 5
2	New Buffalo	G 4
14	Niles	G 4
4	North Muskegon	E 4
4	Northville	p15
3	Norway	C 3
6	Novi	p15
37	Oak Park	p15
2	Ontonagon	B 1, m12
4	Otsego	F 5
17	Owosso	E 6
3	Paw Paw	F 5
3	Plainwell	F 5
9	Plymouth	F 7, p15
82	Pontiac	F 7, o15
36	Port Huron	F 8
3	Portland	F 6
3	Richmond	F 8
18	River Rouge	F 7, p15
7	Riverview	p15
5	Rochester	F 7
2	Rockwood	F 7
5	Rogers City	C 7
3	Romeo	F 7
4	Romulus	p15
3	Roosevelt Park	E 4
50	Roseville	o16
81	Royal Oak	F 7, o15
98	Saginaw	E 7
5	St. Clair	F 8
77	St. Clair Shores	p16
3	St. Ignace	C 6
6	St. Johns	F 6
12	St. Joseph	F 4
3	St. Louis	E 6
19	Sault Ste. Marie	B 6
6	South Haven	F 4
3	Sparta	E 5
2	Spring Lake	E 4
9	Sturgis	G 5
7	Swartz Creek	F 7
7	Tecumseh	G 7
7	Three Rivers	G 5
18	Traverse City	D 5
18	Trenton	F 7, p15
3	Vassar	E 7
3	Wakefield	n12
3	Walled Lake	o15
89	Warren	F 7, p16
16	Wayne	p15
3	Whitehall	E 4
2	Whitmore Lake	F 7
2	Wolf Lake	E 4
44	Wyandotte	F 7, p15
21	Ypsilanti	F 7, p14
4	Zeeland	F 5

Lambert Conformal Conic Projection
SCALE 1:2,347,000 1 Inch = 37 Statute Miles

MICHIGAN

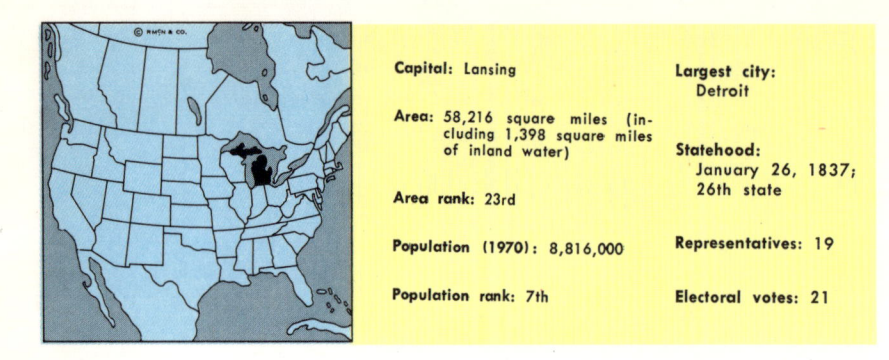

Capital: Lansing

Area: 58,216 square miles (including 1,398 square miles of inland water)

Area rank: 23rd

Population (1970): 8,816,000

Population rank: 7th

Largest city: Detroit

Statehood: January 26, 1837; 26th state

Representatives: 19

Electoral votes: 21

Michigan is made up of two large peninsulas, its shape governed by the shorelines of four of the five Great Lakes. The southern end of the Lower Peninsula is a densely populated industrial and farming region, including Detroit and its suburbs. It has a growing season five to six months long.

By contrast, parts of the Upper Peninsula have a growing season of barely three months. Most of it is a forested wilderness inhabited by deer, bears, beavers, and porcupines.

The first Europeans to see Michigan were French fur traders. In the early 1600's, they paddled birchbark canoes up the Ottawa River from Montreal. French missions and trading posts were established at Sault Ste. Marie and on Mackinac Island.

Michigan had few settlers until after the War of 1812, when settlers began traveling west on the Great Lakes. Landing at Detroit, they laid out pioneer farms in southern Michigan. Then settlers began following the railroads into the prairies, and Michigan was by-passed for a time.

When Michigan became a state in 1837, only the southern part was settled. In the 1840's, iron ore was discovered near Lake Superior. By this time iron was needed for the booming industries of the East, and the great Lakes were an ideal transportation route, except for a stretch of rapids in the St. Marys River. In the 1850's a canal was dug around the rapids, with locks to raise and lower the boats.

Late in the nineteenth century lumbermen swept across Michigan and cleared most of the forests in a few years. The cleared land was to be sold to farmers, but it is not farming country because the land is rocky and the thin soil is not very fertile. Today the trees of the second-growth forest are large enough to be useful as lumber and pulpwood and are carefully harvested. Moreover, this land of lakes, rock, hills, and forests is recognized now as the finest resort country in the Middle West.

Southern Michigan is still the farming and industrial region of the state. It is a famous fruit region, and its farms produce milk and butter for the cities. From the earliest days of the industry, southern Michigan has been identified with the manufacture of automobiles. Detroit is the heart of the motor region, but automobiles and parts are made in nearly every city of southern Michigan.

The Mackinac Bridge connects the peninsulas of Upper and Lower Michigan. Restored Ft. Michilimackinac is in the foreground.